FREE! LOVE YOUR WORK, LOVE YOUR LIFE.

CHRIS BARÉZ-BROWN

PORTFOLIO
PENGUIN

To those who remember that they have all they need to live the most extraordinary lives and that they are neither too fat nor too old, but just perfect.

Keep shining bright, and when you forget, giggle.

And to those who never forget and help me remember: Harvey and Louli and Sparky.

Without you I could so easily have been normal. Thank you.

PORTFOLIO PENGUIN
Published by the Penguin Group
Penguin Books Ltd, 80 Strand, London WC2R 0RL, England
Penguin Group (USA) Inc., 375 Hudson Street, New York, New York 10014, USA
Penguin Group (Canada), 90 Eglinton Avenue East, Suite 700, Toronto, Ontario,
Canada M4P 2Y3 (a division of Pearson Penguin Canada Inc.)
Penguin Ireland, 25 St Stephen's Green, Dublin 2, Ireland
(a division of Penguin Books Ltd)
Penguin Group (Australia), 707 Collins Street, Melbourne,
Victoria 3008, Australia (a division of Pearson Australia Group Pty Ltd)
Penguin Books India Pvt Ltd, 11 Community Centre,
Panchsheel Park, New Delhi – 110 017, India
Penguin Group (NZ), 67 Apollo Drive, Rosedale, Auckland 0632,
New Zealand (a division of Pearson New Zealand Ltd)
Penguin Books (South Africa) (Pty) Ltd, Block D, Rosebank Office Park,
181 Jan Smuts Avenue, Parktown North, Gauteng 2193, South Africa

Penguin Books Ltd, Registered Offices: 80 Strand, London WC2R 0RL, England
www.penguin.com
First published 2014
001

Designed by Alex Dobbin
Printed in China

ISBN: 978-0-670-92355-7

Contents

notes

Head Stretching

1

OWN IT

No one makes you work. The choice is yours.

We are always free and have always been so. We just forget that, and become trapped by our own perceptions. Yes, we need to make money, but there are countless ways to do so. The job you do is the job you have chosen to do. There is no gun to your head. If you don't like it, it's your own fault. There is no sugaring this pill.

It's your responsibility to make your job as good as it can be, so that you can be as good as you can be.

No one can do that for you.

The opportunity to craft an extraordinary future lies firmly in your hands. Take it.

There is no such thing as a perfect job. It does not exist.

Talk to any multibillionaire, Oscar-winning actor, fashion photographer or beer taster and you will soon realize that every career has its downside. We need to craft our vocations so they work best for us. But most importantly, we need to craft ourselves so that we fit our vocations.

Then we can be free once more.

THE OPPORTUNITY TO CRAFT AN EXTRAORDINARY FUTURE

LIES FIRMLY IN YOUR HANDS

* *TAKE IT* *

WHY FREE?

Work is so much a part of what we do, that we sometimes mistakenly assume it determines who we are.

Our relationship with work is central to our happiness, our vitality and our ability to self-express – to be our true selves.

To feel fully alive we have to make work work for us.

Every day that I work, I grow to understand more about it. And I find that the forces behind it – the forces that drive us to work and shape our relationship with it – are not as they first seem.

For example, does work make us happy? Researchers for the London School of Economics attempted to answer this question by tracking and interviewing 50,000 people over three years using a smartphone technology called Mappiness.

The results were a little surprising. They found that work makes us more unhappy than anything else, apart from being ill in bed.

Alex Bryson, who ran the research for the LSE, observed that people were generally positive when reflecting on the meaning and value of their work in their lives. Yet actually doing their job elicited some personal cost in terms of the pressure and stress they experienced.

Such pressures not only influence our happiness but also can warp us into being somebody we are not – often into somebody we don't want to be.

Getting the right job is not an exact science. Sometimes we miscalculate either what a role will involve or our ability to fulfil it, and sometimes we just don't quite fit in with the company or, indeed, the culture we've joined.

I have had jobs that made my heart soar and let me unleash my own unique qualities in ways I could never have imagined. During those periods my experiences became richer; I had my most meaningful relationships, felt a greater sense of achievement and led a more fulfilled life both in and outside work.

Equally, I have had jobs where I've been counting down the minutes, wishing I was somewhere else and finding ways to make the time pass less painfully. It felt as if each day of my life was being squandered, and that my most valuable resources (time and talent) were ebbing away. Worse still, I knew my precious love of life was being leached from me. My life was becoming meaningless – therefore, so was I. There was no alternative but to head for the exit door.

Life and work are intrinsically linked. They are not separate; they are one.

If we want to live an extraordinary life, we have to make our work equally extraordinary.

When your work resonates with purpose, you jump out of bed every morning, excited by the possibilities the day holds for you. Everything else in your life seems to have a glow about it, and you exude much more personal shine.

My aim in writing this book is to help you feel like that every day. To help you make your work work for you. To feel truly free.

Life and work are intrinsically linked. They are not separate; they are one.

FREE **is written:**

To redress the balance and make work
further enrich your life.

To remind you that you are fantastic and have
the ability to do amazing things.

To show you that work is your slave,
not the other way round.

To help you make work your ticket to
an extraordinary future.

To put you in the driving seat and help
you plan your route to freedom.

THE NATURE OF WORK

On average, we only have 27,350 days on this planet. And 10,575 of those are working days. Time is ticking.

If those days are spent doing something you don't love with people you don't like and/or in an environment that depresses you, it's a terrible waste of life.

For most of us, work is a necessity. We need to earn money to provide shelter and sustenance (and huge HD TV screens, of course). Money makes the world go round, and without it we are stymied. No money means no choice. No choice means no fun. And no fun means a very dull life indeed.

The trap isn't only about money. Our ambitions, our goals, our own sense of identity are also shackled by the chains of work. How can you become the hero of your own life when you're renting yourself out for at least ten hours a day?

Work is like a drug to us. It feeds us little hits of success, friendship, growth, power, recognition. Those hits feel amazing and before we know it we want a bit more. We are all different in our susceptibility to work's seductions, but none of us is immune.

Work is also good for us. It satisfies many of our basic needs. It gives us meaning and purpose. It helps us to live the lives that we choose. It helps us grow and connect with others. However, as with all drugs, consumption can easily turn to addiction.

The Gallup-Healthways Well-Being Index shows that Americans feel worse about their jobs and their work environment today than ever before. They estimate the cost of America's 'disengagement crisis' at $300 billion a year: 71 per cent of Americans work during vacation. Only 38 per cent take their holiday allowance while 30 per cent don't even take a lunch break and 48 per cent believe that their lives have become more stressful over the last five years. I'd expect to find a similar pattern in most developed nations.

Something is clearly out of balance.

Work is becoming less fun and more painful than it should be. Work can take away our shine, resulting in us living a little less brightly every day.

But our problems are not work's fault: 'work' as an entity doesn't exist. It has no consciousness. Work is what *we* do. It is what we *are*.

There is no point blaming work; we have to look at ourselves.

We need to change our relationship with work for us to be fulfilled, engaged and downright magnificent. And we therefore have to change our relationship with ourselves.

That's what *FREE* is about.

We need to change our relationship with work for us to be fulfilled, engaged & downright magnificent.

WE ALL HAVE
CHOICE

Stuart Hogue is the general manager of the Girl Hub, a collaboration between the UK's Department for International Development and the Nike Foundation to help teenage girls in three African countries. He wanted to get a clearer idea of what it is like to be a teenage girl in Africa. Girl Hub are clever at getting insights through real experiences, and this one has stayed with him:

Last year, I spent a day with Emebet, a girl in Ethiopia, learning about her life. She wakes at 3 a.m. to study by the light of her mobile phone so she can start her chores at 5 a.m. before going to school. Her chores include lugging forty-five pounds of water for 500 yards on her back to make breakfast for the family and to do the cleaning. I tried it myself; I had to stop every ten feet to complete the task. She also did the farming for the family because her father had died and her mum was ill.

She sold firewood at the market for about seventy cents a day. What amazed me was that from the seventy cents she earned, she'd spend ten to pay someone to charge her mobile phone so she could study in the dark every morning.

What struck me is that although she had in my view an incredibly tough life, throughout the whole day that I was with her, she never stopped smiling. She was a constant force of positive energy. I know if you put her in the right place, she'd be running the company in two years because she knew nothing other than how to succeed; despite every reason given her to fail.

It is not the circumstances that we find ourselves in that dictate our sense of freedom, it's the way that we embrace them and make them work for us.

Countless privileged people have lived a miserable experience. Plenty of famous actors, musicians, artists and business people alike have had the world at their feet and yet could find no freedom or joy in it. Emebet, however, celebrated the choice that she had made to study by the light of a mobile phone at three in the morning. She worked with the circumstances that she had and loved the freedom to do so.

We all have choice.

WARNING SIGNS

Don't Be a Fantasist

Our brains create fantasies. They aren't too dissimilar to us playing a game like Grand Theft Auto. It's a wonderful distraction and just as addictive as gaming (although hopefully not so violent and disturbing). We can be somebody we really aren't.

This is fine in a game, but not in real life.

So stop now and ask yourself who you *really* are.

What is it that makes you unique?

What is it that you are here for?

Why is now special?

Sit back now and ask yourself: is your work helping you access your own personal genius, and helping you to express what is unique and special about you?

There are plenty of clues about this. We should pay heed to them, but we usually ignore them.

If you wake up every morning in keen anticipation of your working day, then you might want to put this book back on your shelf until you need it.

If, however, something occasionally doesn't feel right in the work you do – or who you do it with – then *FREE* is here to free you.

Read through these lines:

I WORK TOO HARD.

I CAN'T SWITCH OFF.

I HAVE BECOME MY WORK.

I'M OFTEN ANGRY OR FRUSTRATED BY MY WORK.

I FEEL STUCK.

I GET BORED.

SOMEBODY AT WORK REPEATEDLY ANNOYS ME.

I FEEL THAT MY JOB JUST ISN'T 'ME'.

NOTHING NEW EVER HAPPENS AT WORK.

I LIVE FOR 5.30 P.M., FOR THE WEEKENDS, AND HALLELUJAH FOR THE HOLIDAYS.

I FEEL AS IF WORK IS SOMETHING TO BE ENDURED.

I'M NOT HAVING FUN.

I'VE BECOME SOMEBODY I NEVER INTENDED TO BE.

MY BOSSES ARE IDIOTS AND MAKE OUR LIVES HELL.

AT OUR PLACE, YOU JUST CAN'T WIN REGARDLESS OF HOW WELL YOU WORK.

If you find yourself nodding in agreement at more than a couple of these statements, it's time to make some adjustments.

STRAP YOURSELF IN, WE'RE GOING FOR A RIDE

notes

True Essence

2

TRY A LITTLE

HIPPINESS

If you can embrace the perspective that you always have choice, then you will always be free. It's challenging, but the reward is the greatest liberation possible.

One of the traps we fall into is to believe we are all separate and individual and in some ways alone. We see each other as discrete entities with unique personalities and fixed pasts and futures, whose life paths may intersect at times only through the randomness of fate.

Our perception is that we are what we see in the mirror, a physical manifestation, and little more. I believe the truth is very different. So did Pierre Teilhard de Chardin.

> 'We are not human beings having a spiritual experience; we are spiritual beings having a human experience.'
>
> Pierre Teilhard de Chardin, philosopher and Jesuit priest

De Chardin believed we all exist within a spectrum of consciousness. At one end of that spectrum, let's say you are

Jed Bowerman in sales. You're thirty-one, living with your girlfriend, but not quite ready to commit. You're still working through some professional challenges but your boss really likes you, and although you work a little too hard you feel as if you are getting somewhere on the corporate ladder, and that makes your hellish commute bearable. All those things are yours and yours alone.

At the other end of that spectrum, you are part of a single universal entity. Every atom in Creation is energetically connected and, although we may rarely get a sense of it, we have the ability to tap into infinite consciousness – a place where time does not exist, a place where worries and fears do not exist, a place where singular identity does not exist. When connected to that energy, everything is possible and none of our earthly concerns matter.

This is not a new concept.

For centuries, those seeking to raise their consciousness have described their experiences similarly, whether using meditation, shamanism, prayer, fasting, religion, stoicism, or healing.

Philosophers, gurus and psychologists from Carl Jung to Deepak Chopra have described our existence using similar language and a consistent frame of thinking.

This is our true essence.

Although our universality is
hard to prove, it is easy to experience.

Try right now. Sit straight, smile and breathe deeply
into your belly, paying attention to the light above
you. You will notice how easy it is to shift your
consciousness. By doing so you can easily get a glimpse
of how we are anything but Jed Bowerman in sales. We
are far more aware of the possibility around us.

Take your time: it's worth it.

If you breathe and be peaceful for a minute
or two, you will feel a shift.

Jed Bowerman represents what we experience by focusing on
our physical lives and our physical bodies, as opposed to who
we are in essence. The experience that you have at work is just
one element of who you are. If we choose to perceive ourselves
solely as Jed Bowerman, thirty-one, in sales, isn't it likely that
we will be forever trapped? By shifting our beliefs about who
we really are, we will instantly gain liberation.

For some this perspective will be easy to hold, for others it will
be more of a challenge. The point is not how far you can flex but
that you do it regularly so you have more freedom to perceive
and therefore to be. And that goes for all elements of your life
but especially for your work.

Try to adopt a more flexible perspective about your job and how
it relates to you. That means you have far more opportunity to
make your job work for you – and to become truly free.

YIN AND YANG

My agency, Upping Your Elvis, specializes in helping organizations improve their creative leadership. We help people rediscover how fantastic they are, and how to use their individual talents to show up every day with more energy and more confidence to make their own unique impact.

I have spent years working with a wide array of people and organizations, and I've recently noticed clear signs that the business world is changing. And it is changing at a fundamental level.

Business has always been about using intellect and logic. We excel at examining things, and from robust data we extract conclusions about what we should do next. Every step builds towards an overall strategy, and if things can't be explained we will keep searching for an explanation until we find one that fits. This is what I call the 'Yang' approach to business.

The Yang is essential for us to be smart and professional and measured in our actions. It saves us lots of time by applying past experience to today's world. It looks for patterns and trends so we can make sense of what's going on. When we can't explain things, we worry that we are not in control.

This is the Machine-like part of business life.

This logic-based business paradigm has served us well, but it is now beginning to fail. As a sign in Albert Einstein's office allegedly read, 'Not everything that can be counted counts, and not everything that counts can be counted.'

We are starting to realize the limitations of logic when it comes to business. Business is all about people. People are fascinating and unpredictable and exceptional. When we start to believe we can make sense of them through mapping and insight and data, we will often be surprised to be proved wrong.

There is so much of the universe that we must accept we don't understand. There are things that can't be explained and which don't fit into a neat little intellectual model. That's scary. Leaders are expected to have smart answers for everything, but that is no longer possible. (In truth, it never has been.) Yang is no longer sufficient.

'Business Yin' is my phrase for the unseen forces that are every bit as important as those which are more apparent. They include passion, excitement, belief, humanity and friendship, as well as intuition, energy, empathy, consciousness and connection. They are what make an organization, and indeed a leader, exceptional.

These are the Human aspects of business life.

At Upping Your Elvis we believe that everybody is perfect, but they often forget that fact and are unable to tap into it. Our job is to help organizations and the people within them to rediscover that potential, and love every minute of doing so. That may sound fluffy, but in terms of hard cash the return on investment that we help businesses achieve can be incredible. We wouldn't be asked back again and again if we didn't have a genuine impact and add real value to our clients' businesses.

Such a human-centric focus almost always has a far greater effect than any rebrand, restructure, downsizing, strategy shift, process implementation or other initiative the board has sponsored. That's why I have devoted my life to the Yin. Get people to be their true extraordinary selves, and everything else follows.

THE
HUMAN IS
BALANCING
OUT THE
MACHINE

Businesses, and indeed the new generation of leaders, are growing increasingly aware of the limitations of the logical brain. The tide is turning; we are waking up.

A. G. Lafley, Procter & Gamble's CEO, is a strong advocate of meditation and is convinced by its benefit to business. So is William George, a current Goldman Sachs board member and former chief executive of the health-care giant Medtronic. And so was Apple's Steve Jobs. Electronics giant Fujitsu has for many years sent its managers to a Zen monastery to unlearn ingrained behaviours.

Business is embracing a new way of being, and a new attitude to what success looks like. What were once thought of as hippy concepts are now seen as smart and innovative.

The Yin is on the rise.

The Human is balancing out the Machine.

I am not claiming that logic and rationality and analysis and intellect are useless in business. But they are no more than a fraction of our ultimate genius.

Business is changing. A new breed is emerging. Some leaders are shifting the balance from ego to compassion, and from science to humanity.

Many CEOs now realize that measuring things will not provide all the answers. That's because many of the most important things in life cannot be measured. Not all that counts can be counted. Empirical evidence was once seen as the Holy Grail of business; soon I believe it will be seen as marginal. Consciousness is not quantitative. Try measuring love.

READING *FREE,*
FEELING FREE

FREE is a combination of Yin and Yang.

I am not a huge fan of planning things in a linear style (my brain is anything but linear), but I hope my limitations as a writer might actually benefit you as a reader, since they let you choose how you prefer to engage with *FREE*.

There are certainly themes and ideas that build throughout the book, so starting at page 1 and reading to the end is one perfectly good option. But *FREE* also works nicely as a random sampler of inspiration (especially when placed in the bathroom, apparently. I am always pleased to hear that my books work best where we relax.)

You choose what works for you. And enjoy the Freedom.

The book includes some very practical ideas and tools that you can try. These are based both on my experience and on simple trial and error.

They are your Yang steps: logical, simple and easy to implement.

The Yin steps are the balance to that.

They are bigger, more profound, and more energetic. They are harder to make, but will take you further down the road. At times during your journey you might feel hopelessly lost – that is because the concepts you are reading about are vibrating at a different frequency from the ones you are familiar with. If you reread a section and it still doesn't sink in, take a break and a few breaths and come back to it when you feel right.

To shift your consciousness by reading a book is unusual, but it can be done if you truly connect with where it takes you.

Keep breathing, keep smiling, and let the adventure begin.

FOR THE DAYS WE FORGET

Avidyā is a useful concept. The Sanskrit word *vidyā* means wisdom or knowledge; the prefix 'a' indicates lack or absence. Avidyā, then, is a fundamental blindness to reality. The core ignorance isn't a lack of information but the inability to experience your deep connection to others and to your true self.

Avidyā is an ignorance of what and who we are and of the underlying reality that connects everything in the universe. We mistake the temporary for the eternal, the tainted for the pure.

The freaky thing is that we are designed with that ignorance inbuilt. If we were all aware, all of the time, that we were part of an infinite consciousness – and that the nonsense we put up with on a daily basis is all part of an amusing game – we would hardly bother engaging with this human experience. To be fully human, we need innate amnesia.

Even when we do manage to achieve a deep and profound connection to who we really are, it is an experience often fleeting and easily forgotten. Our overactive minds begin focusing on tomorrow or yesterday and the experience of true connection fades.

The only way to overcome this amnesia is to create notes to help us remember that we are amazing and have the freedom to choose how we want to be.

The simplest form of note is a physical one, dozens of which I have littered throughout my life and which range from journal entries to Post-Its on a wall. My other notes include my family (who remind me that there is more to life than toil), music I associate with happy occasions and the view of the sea from my office window.

I make sure I plan rich experiences into my life that will reconnect me to my essence – time spent with like-minded friends, travelling to adventurous places or even one of my more bizarre favourite activities, chopping wood. It all helps me to remember.

FREE will help you create notes. Every day you'll remember that it's your choice to be at work, and therefore your choice as to how you play when you aren't.

Notice that your mind is already wandering. Reread this last section and notice what happens as you do.

Time for a note.

Schedule in your diary a ten-minute meeting with yourself

tomorrow. Use that time to ask: Where am I on that consciousness spectrum right now? Am I Jed Bowerman, or am I feeling bigger than my job, my name, my body?

'Advances are made by answering questions.
Discoveries are made by questioning answers.'

Bernard Haisch, astrophysicist

SOON IT WILL

BE GONE

You have just arrived. You have no past.
You have no future.

One of the traps that we fall into – one that keeps us wedded to the belief that we are finite and discrete – is being led by our wandering minds. In this book we will come to see how minds can work at many levels and can be an amazing source of liberation. But for most of us and for much of our time, they are the problem.

Perception is reality, and therefore learning how to perceive is one of our greatest lessons. Our minds, when we are playing at being Jed Bowerman, love a distraction. Like a child in a toy shop, they will be attracted to anything shiny and new. They find things that are imagined more appealing than the reality in front of them, and they are masters of creating their own worlds, their own fantasies.

What that means is that our minds tend to focus on the past or the future. The past is a beautiful thing because there are many memories that can act as stimuli for the mind to play with and embellish. The future is a blank canvas on which our creative minds can draw no end of fantastical images – we can play without constraint. The drawback of this talent is that it's very easy for us to spend more time fantasizing than living life.

> 'Most people treat the present moment as if it were an obstacle that they need to overcome. Since the present moment is life itself, it is an insane way to live.'
>
> Eckhart Tolle, author of *The Power of Now*

America's favourite spiritual teacher Eckhart Tolle estimates that we spend up to 90 per cent of our time lost in thought. This trap not only impedes our brilliance by distracting us from what is happening now, it also fuels the amnesia of who we truly are. It keeps us well and truly stuck. In some meetings the ability to detach yourself from another boring PowerPoint slide may seem like having a superpower; but the long-term result is growing detached from life.

To help you overcome that trap and free you from its clutches, we need to revisit the idea that we live on a spectrum – and that we see only part of it most of the time. To jolt you out of that stuck and myopic viewpoint, I would like you to imagine this:

Your physical body, in which you believe you reside and which is the major part of your identity, is actually a spacesuit. It is there purely so that you can have the physical experience of being human.

When I say 'you', I really mean 'us'. If at the highest level we are all one and interconnected, then elements of that higher consciousness are what power and inhabit the spacesuit.

These elements have different personalities and energies, and are fleeting.

Thus, the essence of who you are in the human experience is constantly changing – the only permanent thing is the spacesuit. The memories we have are spacesuit memories, and not memories of the true self. They feel incredibly real and comforting because at an earth level they give us identity. But they are no more important to our current reality and our true perception of it than the book we were reading last night or the film we'll see tomorrow.

You may struggle with this concept. I know I did.

You may feel distracted now, or even a bit foggy. Don't worry: that's part of the human experience, and it is symptomatic of what I have just been describing. So take a deep breath and imagine that you have just arrived here, at this second, and that you have no past and no future.

What is true?

What is needed right now?

Whatever realization you have just had, write it down somewhere.

And leave yourself a note, for soon it will be gone.

ALL YOU NEED IS

HERE AND NOW

As we have ascertained, you are infinite consciousness. (How I love writing that.)

You therefore have access to untold smarts, amazing insight and compassion that never tires. You just need to tune it up.

I have been helping people tap into their creative genius for many years and I know that we can all have amazing ideas from any kind of stimulus. All the answers we need are within arm's reach; we just need to know how to look.

During a workshop I was running recently, I sent a group of quite cynical and hardened media executives into my garden. The brief was a simple one: find something out there that grabs your attention and see what ideas it gives you.

One guy, Seb, came back with the most mighty of revelations. He had believed prior to our work that he wasn't creative – he felt all he was good at was logic and analysis. Yet he came back with a breakthrough that was inspired by a molehill.

We had spent the day getting into a more sensitized and tuned-up mode. So when he went outside he was happy to go with the flow, which so often he wouldn't have been.

Seb had a major project ongoing. He was having problems getting it running and had no idea why. When he saw the molehill, his thought process went like this:

MOLEHILLS ARE MADE BY MOLES.

MOLES ARE AMAZING AT DIGGING, HAVE A TREMENDOUS SENSE OF SMELL, BUT HAVE LIMITED EYESIGHT.

THEY DON'T CARE WHERE THEY ARE WHEN THEY ARE UNDER THE GROUND DIGGING, AND NOR DO WE. WE ONLY CARE WHERE THEY POP UP, AND WE DON'T WANT THAT TO BE IN THE MIDDLE OF OUR LAWNS.

He then started to wonder who might be worried about him digging up their lawn. Seb thought about the way his colleagues had been acting and suddenly realized that one of the leadership team, Marie, had been dragging her heels, preventing his project from gaining momentum. Why? Perhaps she was worried that his project would negatively affect her department. He phoned her that night to see if he was right.

When they explored his theory on the phone it became apparent that Marie had indeed thought this, but subconsciously; she hadn't really considered the implications of Seb's project before, and yet her behaviour showed clearly that she was concerned about them. It took some teasing out for her to be able to articulate her fears, but once they were verbalized she and Seb were able to agree a course of action to resolve the problem.

What was most interesting about this breakthrough was that Seb's subconscious had obviously spotted some clues that Marie was making his job harder, and yet he hadn't pursued that train of thought. The molehill acted as a stimulus to allow his brain to release his observations to his conscious mind, so he could act upon them.

If we are in the right state of mind, then any stimulus can give us a clue to what our subconscious (or perhaps higher consciousness) is picking up.

If we are in the right state of mind, then any stimulus can give us a clue to what our subconscious is picking up.

A research team at the University of Iowa asked volunteers to play cards with different decks, some of which were fair and some of which were rigged against them. Their stress levels were monitored by measuring the perspiration levels on their palms. The rigged-deck participants started generating stress responses within ten cards, yet they didn't suspect the game was fixed until fifty hands had been dealt, and couldn't articulate it until eighty. Their clammy hands were giving a subconscious signal well before their conscious brains had made any sense of what was happening.

This might all sound rather 'New Age', but there is so much evidence behind our ability to intuit (i.e. the physical and emotional responses to our subconscious processing) that even the far-from-fluffy US Navy is investigating whether military personnel can be trained to improve their sixth sense.

Troops in Iraq and Afghanistan have reported an unexplained feeling of danger just before an attack, which can help them prepare and therefore save lives.

If this sense can protect us in dangerous situations, it can also help us be more brilliant in our thinking and creativity in business. In extreme situations we tend to receive more resonant emotional feedback from our subconscious. Having ideas isn't dangerous, so you need to sensitize yourself to what's going on inside and outside in order to spot minor fluctuations.

Seb was in a very tuned-in state when the molehill moment came. For you to have the same breakthrough, you also need to tune in.

'No problem can be solved from the
same consciousness that created it. We have
to learn to see the world anew.'

Albert Einstein

If you feel trapped and dissatisfied by any element of your job, the answer to your freedom is near you right now. Slow down, breathe deeply and maybe go for a slow stroll outside. Notice everything around you and really drink in every detail. See the beauty in everything.

Stop somewhere you can relax, and breathe in all the colours and shapes and shadows. Notice the sounds around you – there are layers to them when you listen closely. There are scents on the air that, as you breathe in, you become conscious of; and there are tastes in your mouth.

Notice how your body feels, its temperature, the feel of your clothing on your skin. As you move, be aware of your muscles and bones. Go very slowly. Watch your feet as you walk, and then stop and look up to the sky. Breathe deeply.

When the time feels right, ask yourself what is it you need to do now to become free within your job. What is it that, if you were to change it today, would make everything different for the better? When asking this question, focus on the things that you can control and that relate to you, rather than things that are external to you.

As you breathe, you will know which ideas have more potential because they will have more energy attached to them – they will tangibly produce more excitement in you and your body. It will take a little practice, but you will be amazed how quickly reading your inner thoughts can become a part of everyday life.

It is like a walking meditation. In essence you are slowing down your brain to help you access more of your subconscious, and therefore sensitize yourself to internal processing, to external stimulus and to universal consciousness.

Not bad for some deep breathing and a wander down the road.

UNPLUG

Sir Paul Smith, one of the UK's most revered fashion designers, doesn't have a mobile phone, a computer or even an answering machine. To some he might seem out of step with today's world, but I believe he's really on to something. Of course, Sir Paul is in a privileged position that has been achieved through his talent and hard work, so his staff, friends and family know how to get hold of him. It may well be easier for him to unplug than for most of us, but the principle is still a good one for everybody.

These days it is almost impossible to switch off. Everywhere we go we are bombarded with messages. It was easier to ignore the media when it was static and lived only on your television or in your newspaper, and when you could be out to telephone callers. Nowadays we carry it with us everywhere and it intrudes into our lives constantly.

There is no fighting progress, and neither should we want to, but it has a huge impact on our freedom. Once upon a time when we left the office, our work for the day, or for the week, was finished. That is no longer the case: 71 per cent of business executives even work on holiday, let alone in the evenings and at weekends. The edges are blurring between work and life, which has given us flexibility, but such constant intrusion makes it harder for us to be free.

The distraction of mobile devices and the constant infringement of family life is the cause of many relationship issues. Dads are constantly being accused of being disengaged because they cannot resist that tell-tale vibration and flashing light; mums are equally obsessed as they also want to keep on top of things. So connecting in the flesh is becoming increasingly difficult. The internet is also increasingly becoming the babysitter – not only are Mum and Dad intermittently dipping into their email and their Facebook, but their children are being entertained by the same source.

The average number of screens in a household that can stream video – and thereby keep us plugged into the outside world – is now ten, according to educator Alan Moore in his great book *No Straight Lines*. He also estimates that we look at our smartphones on average more than 200 times per day. Soon there will be no escape.

There are some worrying side effects of this multiscreen, multifaceted life that we lead. When we are multitasking the effect on our IQ is that it drops by ten points, according to research carried out at the Institute of Psychiatry at the University of London. That is the equivalent of skipping a whole night's sleep. Smoking marijuana only reduces it by four points, so all this technology can be more harmful to our smarts than a big fat spliff. (There is some debate about this research, and the drop in IQ is only temporary, but it should at least make us question the detrimental impact that our distracted lives might be having on our genius.)

Of course, using all these screens has improved our visual-spatial intelligence. These are useful skills when piloting a plane, managing a nuclear reactor or keeping patients alive during surgery. But in a recent experiment at Stanford University when researchers tested a group who did a lot of media multitasking against a group who didn't, the multitaskers didn't do well at anything. The researchers expected them to at least have developed some special skills – but that wasn't the case. It appeared that they were distracted by pretty much everything. To make matters worse, the multitaskers weren't even good at multitasking. In short, we are becoming shallower.

'Oooh, butterfly!'

> **'We now have weaknesses in higher order cognitive processes including abstract vocabulary, mindfulness, reflection, inductive problem-solving, critical thinking and imagination.'**
>
> Patricia Greenfield, UCLA psychologist

Although technology can help us do amazing things, we need to be aware of its pitfalls and its effects on us. One thing that drives me nuts is when I meet somebody – professionally or just out for a beer – and the first thing they do is put their phone on the table. What this communicates is: 'Yes I'm sitting here with you, but there is a much more important world out there waiting to get through to me and if it calls I am going to drop you like the piece of crap you are.' That may not be their conscious message, but that's what they mean.

Don't be the arse with their phone on the table. Put the damn thing away.

Even world leaders aren't immune, though at least some are sensible enough to realize it. US president Barack Obama remarked on his fondness for tinkering with his Blackberry: 'Information becomes a distraction, a diversion, a form of entertainment, rather than a tool of empowerment.'

I would never suggest that we turn our backs on all these advances and live by the light of a campfire singing folk songs (at least, not every day), but we should choose our interactions more carefully. We should invite technology to help us when we want it, rather than treat it like a whining child pulling at our trouser legs.

I am a fan of anything that increases our awareness and breaks habits so that we can consciously choose how to use our technological security blankets. Spend a week not doing any social networking and notice whether your life is any worse as a result. Spend five days a week using your devices in any way you'd like, and then for the other two days, switch off your broadband and use your phone as simply a phone (i.e. just to speak to people, like in the olden days). It can be a great discipline to keep your computers and tablets away from communal family areas once work is finished, so you have to deliberately go to them if you need them.

Try leaving your phone in your bag whenever you meet someone, or leaving it at home or in the car if you go out for drinks or dinner. I'll bet you engage more with whoever you are meeting, and have a much more rewarding, fun time.

Accidents occur when people stride along busy streets unaware of traffic because they're busy emailing or texting or listening to music. But beyond the obvious dangers of being constantly attached to our devices, they mean that we aren't smelling the roses and we aren't taking in the richest stimulus available: that of life around us.

I read about an aerospace executive who was on a retreat and was walking late at night without his Blackberry. He looked up and saw the stars and was struck by the fact that he couldn't remember the last time he'd seen the beauty of the firmament. The next morning he awoke worried about what else he might have missed.

Unplug, look up, and see the sky.

By deliberately unplugging yourself, you will notice when technology is useful and when it is not. Then you can deliberately choose when to embrace it, reclaim some of your freedom, and help escape from the 'shallows'.

UNCOMFORTABLY
NUMB

For us to be shiny and free, we need to let our minds process and reflect. The temptation to entertain ourselves for every hour of every day prevents us from having the chance to make sense of all our experiences. We can play with our apps, watch YouTube, trawl Facebook and endlessly consume media from every corner of the internet. There is junk available to us constantly and it tastes sweet as sugar. Our cave-dweller minds love distractions and all this overstimulation feels like Disney World every day.

I was one of the worst offenders because I am a music junkie. Whenever I travelled I would have my ever-so-fancy earbuds in, cutting myself off from the world and creating my own bubble. One day I forgot my tunes, and found I got a lot of thinking done about the more important stuff.

I know I will never throw my music away – it's a passion and a part of my life – but I do now more consciously choose when to unplug and reflect in peace. For me it creates more perspective and allows me to think more freely.

LIVE A MORE TECHNICOLOUR

&

EXTRAORDINARY LIFE

One simple trick to help you escape the bubble and re-engage with the world around you is to carry a small notebook with you. Write down three things a day that you found surprising, unusual, or just plain attractive. Things that made you go 'Ooooooo' and made you feel alive.

By doing this you will programme your brain to spot things more readily, and become more sensitized to the world around you.

The stuff that makes you go 'Ooooooo' can then be stimulus for you to play with.

Ask yourself what it was that made such an impact. What was attractive about it? How could you get it to show up in your life more often?

For example, I find I am mesmerized by waves, and I also feel good doing physical activity that isn't in a gym. Paddle boarding was a simple way for me to combine those two positive reactions.

This technique works in a business context, too. A client of mine noticed that she felt more alive when having to pitch big projects – she loved the pressure. But she had the opposite reaction when she had lots of little projects to run – then she felt distracted and stretched. She has since redesigned her job to always have a big hairy pitch on the go, while she spreads the smaller stuff around the team as development projects.

By noticing your reactions more, you can explore what stimuli create positive feelings in you, and then work out how to get more of them happening every day.

You break away from being a passive receiver of stimulus and instead use it to live a more technicolor and extraordinary life.

'Stop consuming images and start producing them.'

Terence McKenna, psychonaut

WE ARE ALL ONE, WE ARE ALL THE SAME

Judgement is pointless.

I'm not referring to the judgement you need to make sound investment decisions, or gauge the speed of a tennis ball as you strike it with a racket. Or the judgement you need when it comes to recruiting people, developing them and keeping them excited about their work.

I am referring to being judgemental of people. The type of judgements we make that dictate how we perceive people and how we interact with them.

When we are being Jed Bowerman, when we are individual and separate, we see others as individual and separate too and therefore we are almost compelled to judge them. We compare and contrast and see how they match up to our visions of the world and to what we most value. We have become incredibly skilled at this, a little like a farmer who has a morning to sex hundreds of sheep with little room for error.

When we all lived in caves it was vital to be able to decide whether people were friendly or not in an instant, and we still carry that power today. We can judge, label and decide within seconds of meeting someone. We can even do it visually from a distance, so developed is our art. It is a way that we make sense of the world and our position within it. It's one of the ways that our prehistoric brains keep busy.

We are designed with emotional pathways that run directly from the eye to the brain's emotional control centres, bypassing the cortex, so we often react emotionally before we have time to interpret consciously. We then misinterpret that emotional response for a rational one and use it to fuel our judgement. This might have been a great survival technique but today it is more often a burden.

As we are all part of universal consciousness, it would be crazy to think that we could be anything but good in essence. Yes, we may be misguided, manipulated, brainwashed, corrupted, but underneath all that negativity we have the ability to connect back into what we truly are and to remember our true nature. So, judging people is an enormous waste of time.

'If you judge people, you have no time to love them.'

Mother Teresa of Calcutta

When you are judging people you are assuming that we are separate and different. But if you were connected to your true essence, you would not see that separation and therefore you would not be able to judge. I'm not religious, but I think Mother Teresa had it just right.

I appreciate that it can be a constant challenge to remain in that state – to remember that what we are feeling is part of a greater shared experience. But the challenge is what makes it worthwhile. Life is rich because at times we take knocks, we react as a human would when faced with perceived rudeness, difficulty or any number of little bumps along the road.

To remain free we need to notice when we have reacted, take a deep breath in and smile and then let it go. Otherwise, we have fallen into the trap that is designed to make us fret about unnecessary things, to experience negative emotions and to then react in a way that reflects badly upon us.

There are no such things as bad people, only bad actions.

I was recently on the wrong end of an appalling customer-service experience, not once but repeatedly over a twelve-month period. The company in question was BT. Every time I tried to resolve it, it fell apart. The time wasted on the phone was running into weeks. No two departments within the company seemed able to communicate owing to its siloed structure, so I was being shifted from pillar to post with nobody owning my issue. At one point I even got the impression that somehow the bad service I was receiving was entirely my fault!

I was frustrated beyond belief and when I was threatened with court action over an unpaid bill for services I had not received, I did start to lose my sense of humour. But then I caught myself and realized I was trapped in a behavioural pattern that was doing nothing to make me more fun, more shiny and more bright. I was being judgemental, by which I mean I was judging the BT staff I was dealing with.

In truth, though, it wasn't their fault. The systems and processes within BT make everyone's life hell; not just mine but also the people employed there.

To be angry with the people I was speaking to was unfair. They had to experience more pain from those systems than I ever will: they work with them for forty hours a week, while I can always buy my telephony from another provider. I am sure they were talented people with the potential to deliver amazing

There are no such things as bad people, only bad actions.

customer service, but their working conditions prevented them from being as amazing as they could have been. Once I switched my perspective and actually started to empathize with them, I was once again free.

Negative emotions such as hostility, resentment and grievance produce specific hormones including adrenaline and cortisol. At high levels these can lead to cardiovascular illnesses, heart attacks and strokes. Judgement is physically, emotionally, mentally and spiritually bad for you.

Our brains are hard wired to spot patterns and similarities. If our ex-partner was a passive-aggressive bully and we see someone who looks a bit like them, our brain will naturally, and entirely unfairly, impute to that person the same character traits. This kind of snap judgement can block off so many paths of opportunity in our lives.

I love this story from Daniel Kahneman, author, psychologist, and Nobel prizewinner. It's his first memory of wanting to work in psychology and illustrates the point perfectly.

It must have been late 1941 or early 1942. Jews were required to wear the Star of David and to obey a 6 p.m. curfew. I had gone to play with a Christian friend and had stayed too late. I turned my brown sweater inside out to walk the few blocks home. As I was walking down an empty street, I saw a German soldier approaching. He was wearing the black uniform that I had been told to fear more than others – the one worn by specially recruited SS soldiers. As I came closer to him, trying to walk fast, I noticed that he was looking at me intently. Then he beckoned me over, picked me up, and hugged me. I was terrified that he would notice the star inside my sweater. He was speaking to me with great emotion, in German. When he put me down, he opened his wallet, showed me a picture of a boy, and gave me some money. I went home more certain than ever that my mother was right: people were endlessly complicated and interesting.

Notice next time when you start to feel negative emotions through your negative judgements of others – and just step back. Breathe deeply, sit straight, smile and pay attention to who you really are.

When you feel connected to your true self you will also see the person you are interacting with as his or her true self – not as a call-centre worker from BT who has been sent to make your life difficult and who seems to enjoy it, but as part of universal consciousness. When you do this, judgement falls away. If you then open your heart not only will they benefit but you will become free. By no longer being trapped by a negative emotion you can sing happy tunes all day long and feel fantastic for overcoming what could have ruined your day.

And just remember that we aren't our spacesuits. Although, interestingly, 99.9 per cent of the DNA that makes up everyone's spacesuit is identical.

Even as Jed Bowerman, we ain't that different.

THE FLIP AROUND

For those of you who are not enjoying
connecting to your true essence or are finding it
a challenge, here's a perspective to help:

Instead of sitting there and imagining yourself
connecting to your higher self, reverse it.

When we think of ourselves as accessing our
light being, it can feel forced. Instead, imagine the
life force wanting to access your physical body.

Sit and be your higher self, release from your
body and feel yourself free and energetic.
Then notice the desire to connect to your earth
body and you will do so effortlessly.

These connections don't work when pushed,
so by making them in reverse you will find it
a simpler hook-up.

Say great things about folk, you'll get a halo effect from spreading the love.

TALK NICE

If judgements do slip into your mind,
keep them to yourself.

*If you say bad things about the people in your business, your
colleagues will associate that bad stuff with you.*

Bitching and gossiping will only make you look bad.

*Conversely, if you say great things about folk, you'll get a halo
effect from spreading the love.*

*If you do need to vent, get a buddy, make sure you are in private,
and signal clearly that you are having a rant. That way you will
feel better and nobody will be hurt in the process.*

Talk nice, be nice.

LOVE MACHINE

I joined a fledgling innovation agency called ?What If! in 1997. It was the most amazing place where the people believed in the extraordinary. I learned a great deal, ran a fantastic business and made some profound friends. The founders are still close to me, as we shared some rich experiences and we hold similar values.

After being there for a couple of years, we decided the company values needed a re-launch to refresh them. I remember thinking, It's all well and good to be Passionate, Fresh, Brave and create a lot of Action; but you could still be an arsehole. It struck me that what was missing was Love. That became a fifth value and to me the most important as it was truly what made that business different.

Love is not spoken about in business and yet it's a potential superpower. 'What is love?' was the most searched question on Google in 2012. The nature of it is a matter of perspective. In some ways it's pure chemistry, a neurological state that we all have the ability to experience. The ancient Greeks decided that love was too complex to have one definition and therefore they have six different words for six different types of love, the two best known of which are agape (a love for everyone) and pragma (a deep and undemonstrative love that develops between couples over time).

Whatever your definition, love is something we all feel, and

Until you love yourself you can't, truly love others

which provides more meaning to who we are and why we are here than anything else. I am sure when I look back at my life I won't be moved by the amount of work I've done or how much money I've made, but I will be moved by the lives that I've touched and those that have touched me.

We all need love; it makes sense of everything. To be free, we need to love ourselves first. The most common affliction is people's lack of love for themselves. This may be fuelled by worries and concerns about how good we are, whether we deserve happiness, what other people think of us, and even whether we think we are lovable.

Once again the prehistoric brain and its negativity bias can stop us from being whole by encouraging neuroses that stop the energy flowing. The truth is that we are all perfect, and to judge ourselves otherwise would be a crime. When we remember that we are not Jed Bowerman but part of an infinite consciousness having the experience of being Jed Bowerman, then we can see that all these human foibles are part of that experience.

Remember: if everything is easy and harmonious, we learn nothing. The things about ourselves that aggravate us, test us and sometimes frustrate the hell out of us, are all there to help us grow. We must learn to love them.

The single most powerful thing I've ever done in my life was to write down all the things I liked about myself, and all the things I didn't. I then spent time learning how to love *all* of those things, not just the good ones. When I could look at that list and wholly embrace all those aspects of me, especially those I first found hard to love, it felt amazing. I experienced a sense of liberation that has stayed with me.

Exercises such as this can induce a massive energy shift. We exude more confidence but also more compassion. It feels as if we glow. Two days after that experience I met Anna, who is now my wife. I'm sure that if I hadn't learned to love myself she wouldn't have even noticed me, let alone want to share her life with me.

Buddhists believe that self-compassion must come before compassion for others. I agree entirely.

'Love yourself, accept yourself,
forgive yourself, and be good to yourself,
because without you the rest of us are
without a source of many wonderful things.'

Leo F. Buscaglia aka Dr Love

SO DAMNED
EMOTIONAL

Emotions seem to be getting a worse and worse press when it comes to business. Some leaders believe emotions make you weak and therefore there is no place for them at work. That's utter nonsense.

The leaders who think like that are usually scared of emotion and don't know how to deal with it. They do everything they can to avoid the discomfort it causes them. Far from demonstrating strength, this just evinces stunted development; these leaders are emotionally handicapped and so will struggle to do a decent job.

Bless! Send them love and kindness. To be alive and enjoy the human experience is to embrace emotions. For us not to experience emotions would be not to be alive and would rob us of the highs and lows that make our experiences so special. Not only that: emotions fuel our energy.

As I emphasize in Part 4, it's vital to get our physical energy right – it underpins being free – but our emotional energy really ups our voltage. Mira Kirshenbaum's book *The Emotional Energy Factor* suggests that 70 per cent of our total energy is emotional and not physical. For us to show up with the energy that will create our freedom, we need to tap into our emotions.

To be running at full power we need to be sensitive to the emotional energy around us. It's all too tempting to put our heads down, work harder and fuel ourselves with more Trenta lattes so we numb ourselves from the emotions we should be enjoying. If things are bad we tend to plough on regardless and try to get some comfort through judging others, escapism and sugar and caffeine and booze. Repressing emotions can only be bad for us.

> **'Failure to find effective ways to express negative emotions causes you to stew in your own juices and can only be causative of disease.'**
>
> Candace Pert, US National Institute of Mental Health

If we store away an energy that has negativity attached, it affects our overall energy system. The negativity of it can then bubble up in any number of ways through physical, mental, emotional or spiritual channels. Regardless of how it shows up, it is then out of your control and can be a real obstacle to you being free.

If you feel an emotion bubbling up, embrace it. Breathe deeply into what you are experiencing and really feel it. By doing so, positive emotions will bathe you, and negative ones will eventually dissolve. But you have to feel them for this to happen.

When you breathe into a negative emotion, and you have fully engaged in it, sit straight, breathe again and smile and connect with your true self. This emotion is alerting you to what is going on in your prehistoric brain, so you can thank it for bringing your attention to that point, and then let it go. It is then worth spending some time thinking about what judgement you are making or what belief you were holding that was creating this feeling.

Every time we have a reaction there is a lesson to be learned. What is that lesson?

My son, Harvey explained to me this week, whenever he thinks something bad, he imagines the bad thought to be a bubble floating in the air and he pops it with his finger.

Works for him,

works for me.

For the next twenty-four hours
notice negative emotions as they happen.
Behind each emotion tends to be a
negative thought.

Notice what you are thinking and
turn it around; flip it into something
more positive.

If you hold that negative thought
for more than thirty seconds, start your
twenty-four hours again.

notes

Stepping Up

3

DON'T CHASE
THE ORGASM

Jobs are often seen as stepping stones. If I get promoted to level four with buying responsibility, then I can get to level two by the age of thirty-eight. Not bad. The problem with this is that the current job is never the goal and therefore it's never properly enjoyed. It's all about chasing the orgasm, not enjoying making love.

Too many people no longer make love. They focus almost solely on the orgasm and not on the act in its entirety. The goal is to come and, quite frankly, the faster we both get there, the better, because then we can get on with the rest of our lives.

I'm sure that nobody would describe their sex life in such terms, but it is an increasingly common behaviour, at least subconsciously. Some blame wider access to pornography, but I believe that, once again, it's due to a lack of consciousness and our focus upon the destination rather than the journey.

At work it is very easy to be distracted by the outputs. If we work hard then one day we will have the house we want, the holidays we crave and the life we so desire.

When I was young I constantly heard my parents and their friends talk about how glorious it would be to be mortgage free. They couldn't wait for that day to come. I have seen countless colleagues go all misty-eyed when they describe how idyllic their retirement will be: all they will do is play golf and drink fine Médoc. The clouds will be like cotton wool and bluebirds will sing on their shoulders.

This is nonsense. If you can't enjoy now, when you are fitter and younger and more energetic than you will ever be, what are the chances of you enjoying the future? Living in your hopes and dreams is a waste of life. It's good to have a feel for where you are going, but that is purely helpful in terms of how it orients today. Today is what counts. Today is what's real.

Do you obsess about getting that board position? Do you believe that when you get the big car, the fat expense account and countless staff, life will finally begin? You're gravely mistaken. Regardless of the trappings and the role, *you* will still be there.

If you fret about money now you will fret even more when multiples are involved. If you are concerned about what people think about you now, when you have more fame and notoriety it will just get worse. If you don't have time now to do the things you love to do, their pursuit will be impossible with all the added responsibility.

Instead, imagine this. If you learn to lead your life now in the way that you would like it to be led, then as more pressure comes your way through success, you will be much better prepared. The grass is not greener elsewhere and life is no easier for 'them' than for 'us' – it is just our perceptions that make it seem so.

I often hear people saying, 'If only I . . . had their nanny/had their holiday home/was their friend/was prettier/had his budget,' as if the answer to freedom and brilliance could be found in external factors.

Well, it can't.

You can waste a lot of time wishing things were different and blaming circumstances for where you are right now.

The truth is, it is your reality.

You now have to live it.

PAINT THE

PERFECT

PICTURE

One freedom that we all have is the freedom to think, to imagine, to dream. Regardless of your position and how restricted it might be, our minds can construct amazing futures for us.

My father worked on the shop floor of a manufacturing business before he was married. The job was repetitive and didn't require a great deal of intellect. The tea breaks were enjoyable, because all his colleagues were lost in solitary thought for large chunks of the day, so when they had a chance to connect they shared some amazing insights about where their minds had taken them. They were physically shackled to their lathes and drills, but their minds could wander.

We all have an opportunity to think freely. When it comes to careers, dreaming is something we should actively spend some time on. This is not being 'lost in a fantasy'; rather, it is a deliberate, creative action.

Jobs are a bit like holidays: we never know how they are going to be until we start them. We can fantasize about the beach, about the food, about the amazing people we're going to meet. But until we arrive on that Greek island we never really know how the holiday will pan out. That's half the fun.

It's the same with jobs. We need to try to embrace them in order to understand the highs and lows, the challenges, and the places where light shines in. But some decent thinking space will give us a greater chance to get the job that frees us rather than the job that imprisons us.

Take a moment to think back over your life, and identify the times you felt most free. Where and when were they? What was it that gave you the sense of liberation?

Now ask the same questions of your career. When has your work felt exciting, rewarding and fun? Equally, think of the times you have felt most restricted – when it was all going horribly wrong. When you ponder those moments, what themes pop up?

When I search back through my life, the times I have felt most free at work are when I have been doing something new, and when I've had leadership support to help me grow and develop. If people have absolute faith in you, it gives you space to play. I was allowed to try creative approaches to my work because there were no interfering experts who believed they could do it better. There was always risk involved, which I find exciting, and very few rules.

The times I felt less free were when I could easily predict what would happen over the next twelve months and my job was to just deliver. It was all about hitting numbers, and the plan was obvious. Usually my bosses in those periods were interested in their success, not mine.

By looking back in this way, we can get a sense of what we would like to create in the future. So for me personally to feel free, I need a healthy dollop of creativity, I need to be trying something new, I need space to experiment, and I need support from others in my growth and development. Knowing this, I can now set out to design it into my role.

Most of the time we don't need to get new jobs to be free. If we're smart we can make what we already have work better for us.

It's unlikely we can change our roles overnight but we can take on different responsibilities or projects that are more suited to our passions and skill sets. Equally we can try to get rid of some other things that weigh us down and sap our energy, by sharing them out across the team.

When you think about your ideal role, what pictures come into your head? What are you spending your time doing? How does it give you the energy to be extraordinary?

And how are you going to make it happen?

If we're smart we can make what we already have work better for us.

INTERVIEW
REGULARLY

Once upon a time a job was for life, and such loyalty served a purpose for both employee and employer. That was a different era.

The average tenure for a job is around 4.4 years, and if you are aged between eighteen and thirty-six that drops to below three years. We all know that employment does not guarantee security because we've seen so many of our family and friends lose their jobs. Subconsciously we are all becoming 'free agents'.

A free agent is somebody who is less shackled to their identity in their job and is more aware of the opportunities open to them. They are happier to move when the time is right and are streetwise enough to know that no job is for ever. Being a free agent does not mean that you do not care about the company you work for – or indeed that you are only out for yourself – but it does mean you are savvy enough to know the world is changing fast. You must be prepared to change with it.

One way to make sure you feel free is to act free. A simple act of freedom is to go for interviews for other jobs even though you do not necessarily need them. When you interview, it keeps you on your game. You have to show up as the shiny version of you, and, as people assess you, you will assess yourself and see more clearly who you are and what makes you special. You will get better at articulating your qualities.

You will also introduce more stimulus into your life, and have more choices available to you in both the type of job you want and the type of business you want to work in. It's no longer a fantasy because you are actually engaged with interviews, and that helps you make better decisions. Even better, by interviewing regularly you are opening possibilities in your life. Who knows: one of these interviews might turn out to be an incredible opportunity you cannot turn down. By exploring them at least you'll know.

You will also know that if things are difficult in the job you have, you can always do something new – that in itself is a liberation. Do not interview every week for jobs you don't want, but always have one that may be interesting on the radar; at least a few a year. It's not a distraction – it's a little bit of energetic candy. Having options boosts confidence, and confidence helps you reclaim more of your freedom every single day.

**Here's some advice on
interviews from *Esquire* magazine:**

Wear a suit, and a tie, and
shoes that were shined that day.

Don't be late. But don't be too early,
either. Six minutes, max. Any more and you
become an interrupting weenie.

What to carry: a notebook and a pen in your
breast pocket; your résumé (even if they already
have it); mints; a little confidence.

Don't bring a briefcase. No reason you'd need one,
except to try to look important. Also, if possible, avoid
wearing an overcoat. One less thing to worry about.

Stand, don't sit, in the waiting area – less fussing
with yourself when they come to retrieve you.

If it's not obvious where you should sit for the
interview, just ask. Try something like,
'Where's a good place for me to sit?'

When you speak, tread in the waters that lie
between the shores of braggadocio and self-
deprecation. Which means that you can toot your
own horn a little. Never assume someone has
memorized your résumé. Or looked at it.

The same day: mail a thank you note.
In the mail. The actual mail.

THE MONEY
STUFF

Money issues have heavy baggage attached to them, so I write this with a little trepidation. Everyone's relationship with money is different, but it is usually loaded with emotion and firmly held beliefs. There have been countless research projects and countless books written about our relationship with money and they draw countless different conclusions.

The truth is that money is important.

Money is at the core of our very existence. On this planet money buys us stuff that we need to live. It buys us shelter, food and clothing. But it also buys us choice, and choice is a part of freedom.

It's very easy to believe that if something is good, a lot of it is even better. I know many people who think one beer is good, so ten must be fantastic. But it's not necessarily true. Taking a dog as a pet may well have an incredibly positive effect on your life, but my guess is that a hundred dogs would be very detrimental indeed. Is it the same for money?

There is evidence that suggests that money does not buy happiness. As the great Richard Bandler, one of the inventors of neuro-linguistic programming and wearer of fabulous black leather jackets, has said: if you can't enjoy one dollar, what's the chance of you enjoying a million dollars?

Happiness is a feeling that is generated by a relationship with ourselves, those around us and the world in which we live. That relationship is rarely enhanced by having more money.

However, our satisfaction with our lives can be enhanced by cash. The reason is that money gives us choice.

I am not saying that you cannot be free if you are poor: we can all make decisions about how we choose to interpret the world around us, and that is the ultimate freedom. But having some spare cash opens up more opportunities than having none. The important thing about money is to not get used to having it, and not to be handcuffed to it.

Careers often have an implicit drive for more. The next promotion is not just about a bigger office and nicer car and more influence on the business, it's about a more generous remuneration package. We feel we need more because that is the design of the machine. If we aren't hungry for more the whole system falls apart. Ambition keeps us striving and working hard. Yet if you were to reach the point where you knew you had enough, it would take pressure off you and create a great sense of freedom.

We all know people with lots of cash who cannot enjoy it. Money becomes a burden to them because they take on extra overheads: houses, cars, staff, polo ponies . . . Before you know it they need a couple of million a year just to keep it all running. There is no fun in that.

There *is* fun in having some cash to play with, because there are some things that we can buy that will really make us feel free. Experiences.

Experiences help you feel more free than if you simply acquire more material possessions. These experiences can be anything at all from adventurous holidays to wine-tasting courses to giving a busker some money in return for their music.

Experiences are what this life is about: invest in them and you will truly be living free.

PRECIOUS TIME AND SHARING

We can always make more money, but time is finite. The more we can make of our time, the more chance we have to live freely.

One of the joys of money is you can choose how to spend it, and one of the most satisfying things to spend it on is others. That may mean treating family and friends or it may mean helping people who really need it. But by offering your money generously you are expressing a very individual freedom and one that will make you feel good.

Real freedom comes from relaxing your relationship with cash. If you feel you need lots of it to be happy you will never be free. You'll have to continually advance in your career so that you can earn more so that you can pay more. Instead, teach yourself that actually you don't need so much. The air will smell sweeter.

MONEY IS NOT THE ROOT OF ALL EVIL

One message I hear consistently is that as we mature we start to understand what is of real value. Those things can be appreciated at very little cost. Indeed, they are rarely actually 'things': rather, they are moments.

'Many people overvalue money but undervalue time.'

Elizabeth Dunn and Michael Norton, authors of *Happy Money*

MORE IS NOT ALWAYS BETTER

A 2010 study by Daniel Kahneman and Angus Deaton is one of many to have found that there is a threshold of wealth beyond which further increments in income have no impact on the way we feel. One explanation for this is that the richer we become the harder we find it to enjoy everyday experiences that come free. So it appears that money can help you feel more free as it gives you more choice, yet the striving for it can take your freedom away.

There is a happy balance which is about learning to know what you need, and making sure that you still enjoy the simplicity

SEE IT AS A CONTRIBUTOR TO FREEDOM

of life – the joys that don't cost cash. Yet you can still have some floating funds that you can use to express your freedom by buying experiences, by buying time, and by sharing it with others.

Your job provides the money, but how much do you really need? I bet it's much less than you think.

I recently received a surprising and monstrous tax bill. It was my fault for not spending enough time with my accountants; I managed to whip up a perfect storm by having numerous business interests, some paying in arrears and some in advance. The upshot was that three weeks before Christmas I almost had to sell our home.

Traumatic as it was, once I got on top of it and realized we would be OK, the measures I implemented to get us back on track were liberating. I declared it the year of austerity, and we stopped spending money on anything unnecessary. No trips abroad, no new clothes, nothing for the house, no extravagances. It sounds dull but turned out to be fantastic. We spent no time deliberating on getting new curtains and whether they would match the carpet, and we spent more time on what matters: being a family.

I realized we had all and more than we'd ever need to have the most wonderful life. In the process I saved a fortune so we could get back on our feet. What started as a painful experience taught me a lot. So ask yourself again, how much do you really need?

Money is not the root of all evil, but it can become an unhealthy obsession and effectively imprison us. See it as a contributor to freedom, not a silver bullet for happiness.

GROW YOU

One of the single most disempowering experiences we can have as employees is to feel as if we are out of control of our performance and our development. To be free at work we need to be able to own our future, and to do that we need to be in control of how we grow and how we make sense of how well we are doing.

Progress in meaningful work is a primary motivator. We need it.

Some of the most ridiculous things I see in many businesses are their antiquated personal appraisal processes. I can only assume they are designed to extinguish all hope and make staff feel thoroughly miserable about the work they do.

Back in 1965 the *Harvard Business Review* revealed that performance appraisals don't work. This conclusion was based on a landmark study by Herbert Meyer, Emanuel Kay and John French, Jr, that tested the effectiveness of the staff appraisals at General Electric. Since then numerous studies have reinforced this finding, and yet after decades of research 93 per cent of companies still use annual appraisals.

A recent US poll of almost 3,000 people found that 98 per cent believe their annual performance review is unnecessary. A quarter of those polled were HR professionals, and yet these appraisals still go on.

It's not that staff development is pointless. Quite the contrary. According to the research and advisory services provider Bersin & Associates, organizations with a strong learning culture have 37 per cent greater employee productivity. But unfortunately annual appraisals don't get you there. If anything they wreck it.

And let's not even talk about 360° feedback.

Well, OK then, let's. The disaster known as 360° feedback is a process whereby feedback is collated from peers, subordinates, bosses, yourself and even externally. On paper it sounds great as more perspectives should be more useful, and these assessments sound like a very scientific way to make sure we all learn as much as we can, but frankly most of them are the devil's work. Poorly designed 360° feedback (and most are poorly designed and poorly delivered) can contribute to disengagement, frustration, and downright pissiness. In many cases such processes lead to a decline in performance as well as resentment building towards the company. This is today's equivalent of the ducking stool; it's inhumane and ill conceived, regardless of the outcome.

There are many problems with such approaches, not least the fact the appraisals and feedback usually only happen once a year – around the time of pay negotiations. No wonder there's an extra bristle in the air when we know that our children's education is at stake.

Not only that, but the anonymity of the feedback removes all context, making it at best useless and at worst destructive.

For us to be as fantastic as we can be, and truly be leading our own development, we need to know how we are doing every single day.

Years ago I had the pleasure of working with Dan Walker, who was head of talent at Apple. He was quite a radical and had banned annual appraisals at Apple. He used to go around the company asking people how they were doing. If they couldn't answer that question, well, he would go to their boss and shout at them. He believed that it was the boss's responsibility to make sure that everybody, every day, knew how he or she was performing.

I used to agree that the boss should carry the can, but now I think differently. There are far too many poor bosses in this world for us to rely upon them to tell us how we are doing. If we rely on them, we have given up our freedom. When our learning is in somebody else's hands, it can become irregular and erratic, and it is intrinsically biased. When we own it, we become remarkable and our energy and commitment can go through the roof. It's also incredibly easy to do.

Every time you've done something that you want to learn from – run a meeting, pitched an idea, recruited somebody – ask two simple questions.

1. What did I do brilliantly?

2. What can I do even better?

If you ask these questions every day, you start to learn about the impact you're having. You see where you are a star, and where you could be even shinier with a little buff. By doing so you place yourself firmly in control of your destiny.

That will mean that – if you do have a job in an organization that insists on the antiquated process of annual appraisals – you will be ahead of the curve. As your boss prepares to give you all those pieces of feedback that he has gleaned from asking his three mates what they think about you, you'll be sitting there feeling confident you have a much clearer picture of what is really going on. Instead of waiting in their office for a big surprise about how you have been performing for the last twelve months, you can tell them how you are doing every single week and then ask them for their support in your areas of development. By making this part of your daily practice you will most certainly irritate some people. I really do hope so.

We can no longer turn up to work hoping we can just get through another day by performing as we have done for the last day, year in and year out. We have to own our future; we have to own how we show up to it. If your constant drive to improve yourself makes others around you uncomfortable, tough. It is your right to grow; it is your right to flourish.

It would take a very brave manager to say to anybody in any workforce, 'Will you stop asking how you are doing and just get on with your work?' Or, 'I know you are keen to improve but quite frankly you've just got a job to do.' It would be unacceptable. Without a clear view of how you are doing in delivering meaningful work and improving yourself every day, you are not in control of your own destiny and therefore you are certainly not free.

I have been helping organizations embed creative leadership into their cultures for many years. The thing that makes the most difference out of all the interventions, skills, behaviours, attitudes, structures and processes is when people are liberated to learn for themselves. When they take it to their leaders and demand the support they need to become even shinier. Not only do you have much better information to judge where to put your efforts, it becomes increasingly clear that, when it comes down to it, you own it. And that changes everything.

Many companies will insist on delivering 360° feedback. If they do, don't fight it too hard because it's part of a system that is bigger than you. However, if they do inflict it upon you, insist on capturing your own 360° feedback in parallel to theirs and make sure that the feedback is captured face-to-face. Anonymous feedback is pointless – it has no context and therefore has no power. Real feedback is useful when you can look somebody in the eye and get to understand his or her interpretations of you and your performance.

When gathering any feedback, make sure you break it down into three lumps.

Fact – What is it that I actually did?

Think – What is your interpretation of that?

Feel – What is your reaction to that?

This enables you to be absolutely clear on what is fact and what is interpretation (and therefore is owned by the person delivering it).

If you are asking for feedback every day, make a note of it and after a couple of weeks you will spot certain themes emerging. Some will be things that you do fantastically well, of which it is important to be aware. These are things you can emphasize in order to have more impact at work, and by getting a reputation for doing so you will become freer as your currency increases.

You will also notice there are certain areas that people would really appreciate you getting better at. If they resonate with you and you are keen to put the time in, make those your development areas and ask for support from all of those around you, especially your boss.

If they aren't things that you want to improve, design your role so you don't have to. Working on weaknesses is often a waste of effort, so only go for things that you have passion for.

By owning your development you are showing that you are committed to high standards.

But even better, it buys you more freedom.

TOTAL

TRANSPARENCY

Many of the problems that keep us trapped in business are created by a lack of transparency. By demanding feedback every day we help impart more clarity to our performance, which means we can become more confident in how we are doing and eradicate any little surprises.

It's so much easier to feel free at work when you know how you are doing and everybody else is equally clear on that. If you own that conversation then you are in more control than if somebody else runs it for you. Create transparency around who you are and what your impact is. As long as you are driving for growth and constantly upping your game you will do better as a result.

Make sure you have regular catch-ups with your boss about what's working and what's not. Be overt about what you need to do to get the next promotion/project/development that you want.

In those catch-ups, agree tangible milestones for each and monitor your progress towards them. Then there will be no surprises.

As time goes on, transparency about our performance and our value will be coming to us whether we like it or not. So why not get ahead of the curve and create transparency, rather than having it imposed upon you?

The world is changing fast when it comes to talent management. To illustrate this, look at technology recruitment. There aren't enough developers on this planet for the demand. We need so much code written that the market for good developers is incredibly hot.

Gild, a recruitment specialist in San Francisco, take an innovative approach to helping companies find the best talent. They have created the Gild Score – a way of analysing how good a developer is using a combination of public criteria, including complexity of code written, influence, years of experience, and cost of projects. Their system means recruiters can simply and quickly find out exactly who the best developer is in any language, in any location.

Gild themselves needed to recruit a developer, so they naturally used their own system. They managed to find Jade Dominguez, who was based in Los Angeles and was not actively looking for a job. He had no Facebook profile, nothing on LinkedIn, and would have been invisible to traditional recruiting approaches. He had no apparent higher education or work history and yet scored a whopping 97 out of 100 Gild points. An amazing find for their business and only possible because of the Gild Score.

In effect Gild have created a system that makes talent absolutely transparent. It's easier to do with developers, owing to the nature of their work, but it's likely that with the use of technology there will be increased transparency for all of us. That will increase our freedom to pick and choose the work that we love, provided we are doing well. The flip side is, if you aren't doing well, it's going to be harder to hide.

Time to up your game regardless.

CLARITY

It's impossible to be free without finding clarity.

One of the biggest frustrations that I come across in organizations is a lack of clarity: nobody understands where the business is going, why it's going there or how it's going to get there. It is crucial for us to work to understand how our role impacts the greater goal. We also need clarity about what a great day looks like for us.

Some leaders take a pride in feeding their workers just enough information for them to do the job. This is nonsensical. The more we can understand about how our efforts create value, the more we can do it in our own way and be free to interpret those goals according to our talents.

I once worked for a guy who would drop little titbits of conversation that he would have with the board about who they thought was doing well, where the company was really going, and the deals that were going on behind the big oak doors. This information was destabilizing to the whole department as it came with no context and no direction; it was used to bolster his credibility and to keep his people feeling on edge. Enthusiasm is a better motivator than fear; let people know why you want them to do what you want them to do.

If you are lacking clarity in any way, go and get it. If your boss says there is no clarity, which is often the case, create your own and then get your boss to sign off on your interpretation of how you should be adding value.

The answers that help achieve clarity are these:

What's the company's purpose? Why do we exist?

How will we achieve it – what's the model for success?

What goals will help us hit that and when can we achieve them?

How are we going to behave to make that happen?

What are our values?

What's my role in this and how does it relate to other people's?

How will I know that I have been hitting these goals myself?

What support will I get to grow and be better at hitting them?

What will I get if I do hit them? What will happen if I don't?

What is it about me that is unique and highly valued here?

How do I get your job?

What's the CEO's biggest worry and biggest passion?

Who is the most exciting rising star here and why?

What is it that would make me a legend?

These are the points you need to agree with your boss – then you can take responsibility for delivering on it.

By being vague we stay small and trapped, as we don't know where we can play. If you really want to agitate the system, get clarity from your boss or your boss's boss. Keep going up until something makes sense.

CRAP BOSSES
ARE OUR FAULT

It is tough to lead an organization, a department or a team. There are challenges to it. Yet in many ways it is easier to lead than to be a foot soldier as bosses have far more freedom. Leaders are paid to take on responsibility and to bring out the greatness of the people around them. We should help them to do that.

Three out of four employees say their boss is the worst and most stressful part of their job, and 65 per cent say they'd prefer a new boss to a pay rise. Something is broken.

The more senior people become, the harder it can be for them to learn how they are doing. Staff are often nervous about giving the boss feedback, as they believe it might damage their career. That's Jed Bowerman talking, not you. If you want to be free, you have to help your boss to be amazing. If they are crap, it's your fault.

I come across countless senior executives who behave terribly. When I talk to their direct reports they are constantly bemoaning what their boss gets up to and how awful it is for the culture. And yet when I ask them what they have done about it, the answer is usually pretty much nothing. Occasionally they may have contracted a consultant to coach the boss on how to be more effective, but it hadn't taken root and so they'd just carried on. More often than not they just avoid a difficult conversation and decide it's better to be beaten up than to take the risk of helping their boss to grow.

I appreciate that certain leaders are not up for changing – they may have become so set in their ways and so reliant upon their past identity that it is now almost impossible for them to shift. You then have to choose whether, under their leadership, you can be as free as you want to be, or whether you need to find that freedom somewhere else. Either way, you'll get the liberty you need.

I worked for a business once where the sales director was in that 'old school' camp. He played the 'if you look after me, I'll look after you' card. He was so resistant to me advancing my career that I had two clear choices. Play his game, edge forward slowly and always be his slave, or find a more senior sponsor in brand marketing to get me out of there and never get his support again. I chose the latter.

It worked and I got the role I wanted, but it was risky and I lost a buddy in sales. At the time I wasn't confident enough to have the right conversation with him and decided he was better avoided. I have never made that mistake again. Much better to get the moose on the table and have the grown-up chat.

In truth, everybody wants to grow and everybody wants to have more impact. So although some leaders are tough to get through to, you must not give up. Because of a lack of feedback, many senior executives have little awareness of their impact. If they did, thousands of days of work putting together pointless

PowerPoint decks would be saved the world over. Unless we help them understand their impact, we cannot hold them responsible for doing things that are not helpful, so we have a right and an obligation to do so. If it's affecting us you can guarantee it's affecting the organization.

You cannot guarantee that your boss will take this well. Some are brilliant learners who assimilate feedback effortlessly and adapt in the most flexible of ways. Others visibly struggle. But if we do not give them the opportunity, then we are judging them not worthwhile (and, as we know, we do not judge).

If the leader decides that the feedback is inappropriate, then at least you can have that conversation and work out how best to support them. By avoiding it you guarantee one thing; nothing will change and most likely it will get worse.

So how should that conversation go? Quite simply follow the process of *Fact – Think – Feel.*

Before diving into that conversation, make sure that your intention is good and that you are here to help your boss. This is not about venting your wrath or about jabbing them in the ribs. It's about support to help them get better so you can all do a better job.

Set a clear context: this conversation is about sharing with them some things that you have spotted that could help them have more impact. Let them know that you are not wedded to an outcome from this, beyond that they get to hear it. You cannot solve the problem if you don't agree.

It may go something like this:

Fact: 'The last four times that we have gathered as a team you have arrived at least ten minutes late.'

Think: 'I know you are busy, but the message you are sending out is that those meetings aren't very important and that your time is more valuable than ours.'

Feel: 'My reaction to this is that I also wonder if getting together is so important. I don't really look forward to those sessions, as late starts mean late finishes, and my whole diary gets screwed up as a result.'

As those facts are data points, it's important that you agree on them. How you think about them and how you then feel is your choice and therefore must be owned by you.

Your boss could react in any number of ways.

For example, 'Tough. I am the boss and that's the way it goes. Get over it.' Then you will be much clearer about who you work for and you can take that into consideration when planning your career.

Or, 'What you don't know is that I meet with the MD just before that meeting, and he always overruns, which makes me late.' In which case together you can come up with solutions ('Let's reschedule our meeting to start an hour later').

Or, and in my experience most likely, 'Fair play to you, I have been late recently and I appreciate that doesn't start the meeting well and sends out the wrong signals. I will get there early from now on and would appreciate it if you could help me with that. Thanks for pointing it out to me.'

Regardless of how they react, what you have done is claim some freedom. You have acted to improve the situation and whether your action is valued or not doesn't matter, because you have done what you should have. Whatever happens, you will have learned more about the situation and how to deal with it in the future, and also how to deal with your boss.

It's estimated that crap bosses cost the US economy $360 billion a year. We have to take action to help them improve.

You are in the driving seat of your career, nobody else.

NOT ENOUGH

HOURS

Time is life. We only get a finite amount and it's the currency by which we live. Time can be wasted, time can fly by, but because it is fluid it can be bent and flexed to help us.

Some people have more money, some people have less, and it's often obvious from the way they live. We all have the same amount of time, yet there are some people who seem to make much more of it. They are making the most out of life.

At the end of every year I look back and ask myself what I have achieved. So far my answers have included having children, moving to the coast, marrying, writing a book, setting up a new business, understanding what's important to me, experimenting with a new model of organizational change, and more.

I have a healthy fear of wasting time. I want every year to build upon the last and to somehow be transformative. It's not that those achievements need to be financial or even physical, but I find a sense of progression exciting.

If you look back at the last few years, what are the things you have done that have changed your life? Have a ponder – it's important stuff.

Now with that same perspective, ask yourself what you've achieved in work that has changed your career over the last few years? If you can think of a few iconic things that give you a big boost in energy, well done. If not, I would suggest that maybe you are using your time in the wrong way.

> 'There is nothing so useless as doing efficiently
> that which should not be done at all.'
>
> Peter F. Drucker, management thinker

We have far too many things going on in our lives for us to achieve them all brilliantly. We would go mad just trying. That's why it's so important to decide what is going to make the difference to your life that you want to put all your energy into. As we have seen, by dividing our attention and energy we become less competent and reduce our chances of achieving anything iconic.

So choose the thing that's going to make the biggest difference to your career. And do it.

Tim Smit, of Eden Project glory, believes that the secret to achieving great things is to tell everybody you are going to do it and then eventually you have no choice. If that works for you, shout it from the very rooftops. The important thing is that you decide and then you make it happen.

By doing so you are claiming your freedom. The decision is yours and nobody else's and the impact that it will create will facilitate even more freedom. The more success you achieve, the more freedom you get to play, and we all love that.

We are too easily distracted by the pretty things: the email that just pinged into our inboxes; the chance to look at the company's new brand hierarchy; the research report that gives us insight into all the new trends for the next ten years. Such distractions cause us to manage our energy and our time poorly: $60 billion a year is lost in America through poor time management.

A 2013 Microsoft survey found that most people use 60 per cent or less of their available work time to be productive. So most folk are wasting at least two days out of five. Now we will never be 100 per cent efficient as we aren't machines, but if by focusing upon the big thing you can dial that up by a mere 5 per cent, then you are winning.

We all whinge that there isn't enough time to do the things we want to do: I really want to practise guitar but I'm so busy; I never get to work out because of all my travel; I get squeezed in every direction so I haven't seen my friends in weeks.

Try an experiment to get a sense of how time can be on your side.

Make a list of the four things you wish you had more time for. It could be anything. In my case it was swimming in the sea, learning how to sculpt stone, doing maths with my son and practising for a weekend of busking.

When you have your list, for the next four days wake up an hour earlier than usual, and use that extra hour to do the thing you wish you had time for. You may be a bit more tired, but when I've done it I've gradually gone to bed a little earlier and a lot happier.

After four days you can then choose to make time for those things because they make your heart soar, or you can stop whinging about not having time to do them. Either way, you win.

When you do something you really love or really wanted to do, it reminds you that all these opportunities are available to you if you make them important enough.

It's the same with work. If there is something you would love to do in your job, make it your priority, tell people about it and then make it happen.

If it's big, chop it down into little chunks that you're excited by. If when you think about it you lose energy, then ask yourself what beliefs you are holding in your head about that project that are weakening you. How can you flip them round and get turbo charged?

Freedom is nothing unless we do something with it.

Step up and claim it now.

VERGADERZIEKTE

Vergaderziekte. What a wonderful word that is. It's Dutch for 'meeting sickness' and I would wager that it's something we all have experienced. When it comes to freedom, meetings can produce the antithesis: a warm and cosy jail from which there is no escape.

We recently ran some research in a large pharmaceutical company and found that those who attended meetings believed that only 38 per cent of the time they spent in them was productive. Imagine not only the cost to business but also the cost to human spirit.

Some people love meetings. They see them as social events where the refreshments are better than at their desks. It's amazing how days can fly by when meetings are involved; the weekends approach more quickly when you have a diary full of them.

Of course there are times we need to meet together at work. But we must choose them carefully and make sure that when we do, we own them. Regardless of whether it's your meeting or not, to be free you need to own it. What that means is making sure that you and everyone else is clear on why this meeting is important and what it has to deliver. If there is no clarity, ask for it. If people don't know, create it together.

When the scheduled time is up, leave. And equally, if you've done what you need to do, go, regardless of time. If people are unclear of their roles and behaviours within that meeting, drive for clarity again. If no one is leading it, you lead it. If it looks as if something isn't working, say so and be prepared to suggest how to make it better.

Before ending any meeting, let the person running it know what they did brilliantly and what could be even better (following the *Fact*, *Think* and *Feel* approach from page 86). Most importantly, only go to meetings where you have a specific role, when there is a specific outcome that seems of value to you, and which sound like fun. Otherwise, avoid them and get on with some work instead. If there are lots of meetings wasting your time, send a colleague in your place.

If you attend a meeting that seems particularly pointless, offer to run it next time. By doing so you can test its worth by setting it up clearly and getting the energy right. When a meeting ends early, you can do an autopsy and discuss its merits, which will result in either a redesign or doing away with it.

Either way, things will have moved forward and you will have gained some more freedom.

PRISON BREAK

We've always known that *where* we work has a big impact on *how* we work.

The environment around you is not only responsible for stimulating the majority of your thinking but also has a massive impact on your state of mind. Studies used by Johnson Controls have shown that improving the light, the comfort, the air and the ambience in a workplace can increase productivity by 16 per cent and job satisfaction by 24 per cent.

If you are desk-bound for most of your day, adapt your space so it works for you. The more you can stamp your mark on it and add colourful visuals, pictures of loved ones, textures, music and one of those little fridges to keep treats in (but not too many), the more it will work for you.

But the real victory is in going somewhere else. In the past week I have been with two separate clients who have started to work from a third space; not the office, not home, but a private members' club. One works from there every Friday to get the space to clear up the week; the other does it whenever he has 'stuff to plough through'.

When I set up Upping Your Elvis, my children were still young but I had no need for an office, so I used the Soho House club. The Wi-Fi works, there are lots of corners you can hide in that have access to power, you can change your office every day (they have numerous sites), a mobile phone ban makes it peaceful, and nobody is hurrying you off. You get real time to think.

That was perfect for me in the mornings. In the afternoons I would switch modes and meet people or get on the phone, so the rhythm worked.

You don't need to join a fancy club (although it is a nice option). Everywhere these days has Wi-Fi. Use coffee shops, libraries, hotels, parks or pubs, whatever works for you; and, importantly, vary your location. If you use the same places, they eventually become less stimulating, just like sitting at the same desk every day.

There is nothing like the freedom to choose where you work. I love to vary my environment depending on what it is that I'm doing. If I am having a big ponder then I need lots of space, expansive vistas and room to stretch my legs. But if I'm among the weeds doing lots of detail, I am much better off at a desk with screens around me and little interference.

By going somewhere else, we keep stimulated and find the right environment for the work we have to do. And as a National Sleep Foundation poll found, moving when we work helps us sleep better and therefore maintain a better overall state.

I am a believer in working from home if you have the right environment and know how to do it. When I do so I manage to reap many benefits. First off, I get to hang out with my family more and that makes me a nicer human being. There is nothing like being there for breakfast when all too often I am gone before anyone else is awake. It feels like skiving and I love it.

Secondly, I work much more efficiently at home. Once I have overcome the temptations and distractions, I get a lot more done. There have been numerous studies of the impact of doing so, including a well-cited one from Stanford, which have shown the benefits include fewer breaks and sick days, higher productivity (measured as a 22 per cent increase in some cases) and improved work satisfaction. Even a sceptical survey from California State University that was seemingly commissioned to discredit this laissez-faire way of working found that the *worst* upturn in productivity was 10 per cent.

There are real benefits to be had by your employer, too. Many organizations including the likes of Unilever are now enjoying a type of flexi-working. Cisco found that they saved $277 million a year by encouraging employees to telecommute.

Clearly, by working from home you gain some freedom that wouldn't be available to you in the office. Your time is more flexible. You choose the tunes that you pump through your system; and there is nothing quite as liberating as that ever-so-important teleconference that you took part in wearing your Onesie.

SOME TOP TIPS ON HOW TO MAKE STAYING AT HOME WORK:

Have a space that you control. Preferably a room where you can shut the door to the outside world that you call your office.

If you have to use a communal space, make sure you sit at a table. Sofas are only good in short bursts.

Avoid distractions but then enjoy them when they are needed. I work well in the mornings and prefer to start early with focus, but in the afternoon I need stimulating, so some guitar playing or a stroll outside or some holiday planning really helps me. Remember you are not a machine!

Choose a spot that has lots of natural light.

Get all the bits you need there. Phones, printers, Wi-Fi that works. Paper, pens, all the kit, otherwise it's annoying.

Have human contact. You will go nuts otherwise.

At the end of the day, pack your work away or else it's easy for it to bleed into your evenings. If you can see work at night, your subconscious is still on it; hide it away.

Enjoy the freedom. There is no point in working at home if you don't enjoy its advantages. Do stuff you can't do in the office. (No, not that . . .)

Working from home all the time is not for everyone, but every now and again we all benefit from working in thick socks with our favourite mug in our hand.

If you are limited by where you can work, at least try to vary it in some way. Swap spaces with colleagues. Work in the canteen for a bit. Change your desk round.

Even small changes can have a huge effect on how we think and feel.

Mix it up and feel the benefits.

CULL THE
COMMUTE

I have plenty of friends who tell me how much they love their commute and that getting up at 5 a.m. gives them more time to ponder their lives and helps keep a good perspective. I have others who believe commuting time is a fantastic opportunity for them to read all those books they so desperately wanted to but never had the time until they moved further out into the country. I believe these are wonderful stories that help them feel better about the pain commuting creates. But I do not believe them to be true.

I now live three hours from London and quite enjoy the train ride as it gives me time to catch up on work, doze a little and indulge in some reading. I do it once or maybe twice a month. If I was doing it every day I would go mad. Commuting is not good for you. It steals precious time from your life, it affects your health and relationships and it is expensive.

Although it may well be difficult to cut your commuting time, it can have a huge impact on your life. If you cut your commute by twenty minutes it will significantly lower your risk of neck and back pain, obesity and a heart attack, according to a Gallup-Healthways poll.

If you crunch the numbers you will be amazed to see the actual cost of your commute. The people at lifehacker.com (which gives regular tips on all sorts of life improvements) have worked out that every mile you drive to work costs you £500 per year. If you are using that money to pay a mortgage at 5 per cent interest, it would make sense to spend almost an extra £10,000 on a house that is one mile closer to your work.

The numbers get more compelling when there are two people commuting for longer distances; for example thirty miles closer to work for a couple would result in being able to afford a mortgage of an extra £600,000. Commuting is expensive.

A Swedish study concluded that a commuting time of longer than forty-five minutes for just one partner makes the couple 40 per cent more likely to divorce. Ouch.

If you have to commute every day, find a way for it to serve you. Cycling has many benefits: it's a great workout, you get to wear Lycra, and it's very cheap after you've bought that beautiful carbon fibre frame. But it's not for everyone because of its sweatiness and the danger of city roads.

See if you can flex your commuting time so that you're not travelling in busy periods as that will minimize the stress and give you more chance to enjoy it. A client of mine in the States used to drive two and a half hours each way to work and invested heavily in audiobooks. The commutes were hellish but she made the best of it and now has an encyclopaedic knowledge of pretty much everything.

The ultimate goal is to reduce commuting hours so that you are freer with your time, energy and health. As Annie Lowrey wrote in *The Economist*, 'When people say "my commute is killing me", they are not exaggerators, they are realists.'

'I cannot make my
days longer, so I strive
to make them better.'

Henry David Thoreau

FLEXITIME, FLEXILIFE

Along with more flexibility about *where* we work, there is a growing trend for flexing *when* we work.

In Holland one out of three men works part-time and there is evidence to show that this helps everybody. Many companies are now allowing people to put in their hours when they want to and also to choose the amount. This is helping people have more freedom in how they live their lives while providing for themselves and their families. By putting in some extra hours Monday to Thursday, many people are having a longer weekend. Again, this isn't for everyone, but it's nice to have the choice to decide whether it fits for you.

There are plenty of people who believe a 20 per cent decrease in pay is worth 50 per cent more time with their families and their passions. It is an option increasingly feasible in all walks of life. You need some discipline and structure to make it work, but it can be a beautiful thing.

Job sharing is on the rise. Originally it was used to keep senior women in business while they had families, and to enable companies to cut overheads when needed, but now apparently even the Queen and Prince Charles are getting in on the act.

In reality, no job is ever truly full time. We work with the energy we have. For some it's 24/7 and for some it's a couple of hours a day. A clever way of balancing things out is to distribute the load by partnering with someone else to deliver: job sharing not only adds to flexibility, it helps reduce the burden and stress of work.

The other growing trend is for people to have more than one job. Most of the people I work with are self-employed but contract out to numerous different operations at the same time. This is the ultimate in flexibility and in freedom. It keeps you fresh and on your game, as nothing is guaranteed and you are only as good as your last job. Freedom has a price, but it's worth it.

Traditional employment, as it was, will become increasingly rare. We work better when we get rewarded for the work we do every day or every week, and have the freedom to plan how to deliver it. Companies are realizing this and are becoming more accommodating. It can help cut overheads, increase motivation and attract better talent.

In an ideal world, we would all be contractors and self-employed. We would bid for the jobs we want and have absolute transparency about our skills and aptitude so it would be easy for employers to decide who can do what best. If we do a job well, our value goes up; if we do a job shoddily it goes down.

This actually used to be the system in everything from shipbuilding to automotives and still happens today in lots of industries where the labour isn't highly skilled and/or workforces aren't organized, such as agriculture, though often it is based upon favouritism and cost, which is neither fair nor elegant.

To introduce such flexibility to more professional and technical workforces we will need more systems to help us manage the process, like the previous Gild example. And we will need to learn many new skills. But it is coming our way.

Today we have more freedom than ever when it comes to how we work and where we work. Break those old paradigms and create a life that works for you.

notes

Spacesuit

4

FEELING GOOD

Think of your physical body as a spacesuit.
It is there not as the major part of your identity
but purely so that you can have the physical
experience of being human.

To be free, we need to feel good. One of the simplest ways to enhance those positive vibes is to look after your spacesuit. Although we have many energies available to us, our physical energy is fundamental. If we get that right, everything else becomes so much easier.

I am not going to start preaching about cardiovascular exercise, triathlons and blood, sweat and tears; that's not my thing. Too many people get into exercise and overdo it; then either it becomes so painful that they reject it for ever, or they get so obsessed that they do themselves more harm than good. I'm a firm believer in a healthy balance of nutrition, exercise and rest.

Every few years I book myself in for a major personal MOT. My last one ended up with me being examined by a man widely regarded as the UK's most eminent heart specialist. He had a few concerns and therefore ran a gamut of very clever check-ups. My wife and I were summoned to hear the final verdict and the good doctor explained that I was in tip-top condition and there was nothing for us to worry about. I was, of course, relieved, but my wife looked shocked, and protested that I couldn't continue to get away with it. 'Surely now that Chris is in his early forties, he should start running?'

'Goodness, no,' he said with a smile. 'That would be a terrible idea: get a dog instead.'

I love my doctor for that.

If we can opt for healthy choices every day that are attractive and fun and offer a cumulative benefit, we have a much greater chance of sticking to them and making lasting, long-term improvements to our health. There is so much simple stuff that we can all become a little more aware of and which over time will have a significant effect on our wellbeing.

First off, like the man said, get a dog.

Even if you've had a bad day at work, your dog will still think you are amazing and your self-esteem will be buoyed every time you walk in the door. As a friend of mine says: 'If only I was half the man my dog thinks I am!'

Your dog will also guarantee that you get some exercise.

By making sure you are out in nature, walking your dog regardless of the weather, you will feel freer and your ruddy, fresh-aired complexion will make you look great. What's not to like? I've just been out with my spaniel, and I feel aglow. I've now got much more energy to throw into my next bit of writing. There's nothing new about this, of course, but age-old wisdom gets age-old for a reason.

My team runs intensive week-long retreats. These can be incredibly draining on our energy levels, but when I ran one recently it left me feeling better than ever. When I thought about why, I realized it was because I'd had a long walk on the Monday, played tennis on the Tuesday, swum in the cold English Channel on Wednesday and drunk fine claret on the Thursday (oops!).

Make sport social. We don't like letting our friends down, so a tennis four or a game of five-a-side football will help you commit to playing.

Give time to your body in a way that's fun and easy, you will feel fantastic

Exercise that achieves numerous goals will feel easier. My love for chopping wood is not just about the physicality of it, but it keeps my garden tidy and it gives me fuel for my fires, both of which I find deeply satisfying.

Do stuff with your family. My eight-year-old son does press-ups and sit-ups with me every day. The fact that he likes it makes me do it. Get away from your desk and do something physical.

My friends who cycle to work are super fit, and talk about how grounding that time is for them. Exercise such as this doesn't need to be diarized as it happens twice a day by design.

If I take a long-haul flight I book in a massage on the other side to help ease out the knots and tune myself up. It's a routine that helps me travel better.

I was recently at the headquarters of the drinks giant Diageo and thought it was terrific that the gym there was full all day long. In the company there is no judgement about when you exercise as long as you do it. I am used to seeing that at Nike, but it's great to find a drinks company also encouraging such a healthy attitude.

DO SOME STRETCHY STUFF

A hundred years ago 1 per cent of the working population had a sedentary job; today that figure is 80 per cent. We all spend too much time sitting down and not enough time moving. As a result our bodies become less flexible and start to form bad habits.

I often see people who are old before their time. They seem to have shrunk, and now with every step they take they are no longer just fighting gravity, they are also fighting themselves.

There is no reason for us to age prematurely, if we just keep ourselves moving. Yogis say that our true age is reflected by the flexibility of our spine.

The other benefit of some stretchy stuff is that those cave-dweller reactions we experience store emotions within our bodies. By stretching and breathing we can release those emotions and in

In developed countries, more people died in 2012 from diseases related to a sedentary lifestyle than from smoking the process do ourselves a world of good. Emotions that are left to fester will somehow resurface in a way that is detrimental to your freedom. Get it out and you are free.

The number of Americans who practise yoga has increased by nearly 30 per cent in the past four years. It seems we are becoming more aware of the benefits of moving well.

There's plenty of stretchy stuff to choose from, but whichever you pick has to feel right for you. Whether it is yoga, Pilates, static, dynamic, ballistic or even some proprioceptive neuromuscular facilitation (whatever that is). Just try some and see what your body says.

I often get tight in my lower back and shoulders, so I know the moves that keep me free through experimentation and from hanging round in ashrams. Get some guidance from a physio, Pilates instructor, or yogi, and design some stuff that works for you. (Natalie in Lyme Regis is a demon!)

If you're feeling lazy, ask someone else to stretch you. Thai massage works a treat.

BE GRATEFUL

It's all too easy to take for granted things we should be thankful for. To many folk, when running their life at such a fast pace, gratitude can feel a little unnecessary and even antiquated.

But when we were closer to nature and the fate of our crops depended on powers far greater than our own, gratitude was a part of who we were. I believe that should still be the case today.

Some groundbreaking work by doctors Michael McCullough of the University of Miami and Robert Emmons of the University of California, Davis has shown that expressing appreciation and genuine thankfulness improves health and wellbeing.

Just writing down at the end of each week the five things it brought for which you feel most grateful will help you sleep better, exercise more, experience more positive emotions, progress towards personal goals more quickly and also help others more often.

So gratitude is not simply a 'nice to do' but something that deeply impacts our energetic system, which in turn helps us to be free.

Have a quick ponder about all the things you are grateful for right now.

Write a list.

At dinner with your family, get into the habit of asking what it was that happened today that was fantastic and it will make you all sensitive to more positive vibes.

If you appreciate special moments in your life, you will notice that they happen quite regularly.

FEED ME!

To work well, we need energy. On some days we have real bounce and vigour; on others we seem far flatter. That energy will dictate how well we perform and how well we feel at work.

I became aware of the difference food can have on my state when I reached adulthood. Up until that point I seemed to be able to feed myself pretty much anything – as long as it was fuel, I was invincible.

In my twenties I started to notice that what I ate affected how I felt. At the time I was starting to move away from beer and curry, and also to explore Reiki and shamanism, which heightened my sensitivity.

For many years I used to fast regularly. After an experience in Thailand where I drank only coconut juice for a week and underwent twice-daily ritual colonic irrigation (yum), I couldn't get over how amazing I felt. I had lost weight, the whites of my eyes were bright and clean, my nails were stronger, my sensitivity to everything around me had increased and I felt more in tune with myself and the world. My prehistoric brain was behaving.

From that day on I fasted for two weeks every six months, taking only some herbs and drinking some fresh juice. It had the same marvellous effect. The only problem was that it didn't last. I had designed yet another extreme activity into my life and not made it a part of my daily practice. For a week or two after the fast I'd be very aware of how I looked after myself, but the pressures of travel and the influence of mischievous friends meant I would be back to my old ways until the next fast knocked on my door six months later.

Recently I have played with the 5/2 diet. For me the word diet has negative connotations. These days, the sole purpose of a diet is nearly always to lose weight, and when most people lose it, they put it all back on with interest. But I am interested in the 5/2 diet as a way of life that could potentially bring long-term health benefits, improve my energy and make me more conscious of what I put into my body.

The first time I came across it was on the BBC *Horizon* programme that was hosted by Dr Michael J. Mosley in the summer of 2012. He found over a six-week period he lost 25 per cent of his body fat, his blood glucose levels dropped dramatically and there was a halving of his IGF-1 level (the presence of which speeds the ageing process). This is impressive for a regimen that is so easy to implement. The way the 5/2 diet works is simple: you eat normally for five days out of seven and on the other two days you restrict your calorie intake to 600 calories for men, 500 for women. It's simple to do and it doesn't leave me feeling hungry or weak; in fact, if anything I look forward to those reduced-calorie days as I feel more alive and more vibrant.

What I like about this approach is that it's a way of life – something you can do every week as opposed to keeping it for special occasions. Of course, it won't suit some; if you have an eating disorder I would certainly avoid it.

So try the 5/2 for six weeks and notice the difference. You have nothing to lose but a few pounds and that craving for midnight ice cream topped with Parmesan.

Bread. We eat far too much of the stuff. It's a cheap way of filling a hole and it's convenient when you're on the move – in fact it's tricky to buy food on the run that isn't bread-based. But bread can make many of us sluggish or have even worse effects.

Modern hybrid wheats are 30–40 per cent poorer in minerals than forty years ago. Much of that lovely freshly baked bread has been frozen as part-baked dough at minus nineteen degrees Centigrade for up to a year. Today's 'baking' is often little more than the shop staff flicking a switch.

These days everyone seems to be gluten intolerant, so maybe cutting down on your loafage would be a good experiment for you, too.

Try spending seven days not eating bread and notice the difference in how you feel.

I have cut out yeast from my diet altogether and – beyond the pain of missing a fine pint of ale – I feel brilliant. It's well worth a go, especially if the 5/2 is a little ambitious for you.

I find that changing my diet makes it much easier to connect to my true self. The rubbish that we often eat, linked with a comforting routine, can keep us locked unconsciously into a certain perspective. By breaking those habits it is suddenly easier to remember who you truly are. You'll find fresh perspectives that provide more freedom, more energy, and more fun.

'If it has an advert, don't eat it!'

Boy George, singer and reformed bad boy

THE POISONS AND THE DRUGS

Too often we rely on stimulants and all the things that make us feel better by taking away some of our pain. There are some rather insidious drugs that are perfectly acceptable in today's society, yet can have negative consequences on your life and on how free you feel. By definition an addiction is something you don't have control over, and a bad habit can be just as damaging; by questioning a few of your behaviours you can reclaim a lot of your freedom.

Let's start with coffee. There is nothing wrong with a coffee every now and again. I really enjoy the flavour of a great espresso after a meal. There is also some research that suggests a little coffee every day can be good for you physically.

But the danger of coffee is that it is fuelling altogether too much of our working day. It is by far the world's most popular drug-delivery system.

Here are a few facts:

In Britain alone we spend over £120 million a week on our caffeine fixes.

Americans consume more than 150,000,000,000 cups a year.

Starbucks were concerned that a 24-ounce option was just not enough. So they launched the Trenta, a 30-ounce beast that is slightly larger in size than your average wheelbarrow.

A survey of 10,000 working Americans found those aged eighteen to forty-five spent an average of $25 a week on coffee while at work, compared to an average of $40 a week on lunch.

What's driving this addiction? Quite simply, we believe that we perform better with it. When asked, 40 per cent of young workers aged eighteen to thirty-four said they couldn't concentrate as well without coffee. Studies have shown that doctors and nurses are among those who need their fix the most, presumably because of their long hours. So coffee is clearly being used as a drug by those who prescribe them.

Not only that, coffee is used as a reward. When interviewed, 25 per cent of people confessed to buying themselves a coffee as a little treat when work was well done. But whether you drink it to keep you going, to take a break, to provide comfort or as a little 'well done, me', coffee consumption needs to be monitored.

If we get too wired on caffeine it's almost impossible to connect to our higher selves. If we are jittery or anxious, caffeine doubles the feeling. We worry more. Our brains race and become more easily distracted. Often our breathing becomes more shallow, starving us of the all-important oxygen we need and muddling our perspectives.

To make matters worse, many people take coffee with milk and sugar. We are the only species on this planet to drink milk past infancy. (Cats like it only because we've conditioned them to.) Bizarrely, most people have some level of lactose intolerance – the US government website National Digestive Diseases Information Clearinghouse (http://digestive.niddk.nih.gov) suggests that 75 per cent of us have problems breaking down lactose. Yet we quaff it like it's the angels' own nectar.

Again, a little milk is not an issue. I love a bit of cheese. But the volumes involved in a Venti latte can be extraordinary. If you must drink coffee, make it small, black and sugarless.

> 'Most people wouldn't consider packing in a Quarter Pounder from McDonald's between breakfast and lunch. But it's perfectly possible to get more than 500 calories in a Starbucks drink.'
>
> Jayne Hurley, nutritionist, Center for Science in the Public Interest

The fuel that we feed ourselves and the quality of it has a massive impact on our overall energetic state. Next time you feel the urge to reach for that choca mocha latte, take a deep breath and ask yourself: 'Is that really what I need right now?'

Always drink a glass of water before you make that decision. More often than not, *that* is what you actually need.

THE SUGAR

RUSH

To be free, we have to feel good about ourselves. That means feeling healthy and vital and being able to manage our energy and our connection to our true selves. Sugar can scupper all of that. If you want to feel physically and mentally good, then stop eating refined sugar.

Sugar isn't known as 'the cocaine of the food industry' for nothing. According to brain scans, the two are equally addictive. The sugar rush we get when we consume something containing refined sugar is literally a 'high': a beta-endorphin rush similar to the feel-good response you would get from taking opium. The good news is we are buying fewer bags of sugar every year. The really bad news is the increase in what's known as 'invisible sugar' within the foods that we buy every day. The average Western diet includes at least twenty-two hidden teaspoons of sugar each and every day, which means we are eating a horrific pound and a quarter per person per week (a massive 31 per cent increase since 1990).

Robert Lustig, in his book *Fat Chance*, places the blame for obesity squarely on sugar. He believes that it should be regarded as a poison as it not only causes heart disease and cancer but also is to blame for the recent massive worldwide rises in cases of type II diabetes and obesity. Between 1980 and 2011 the world's diabetic population has more than doubled to 366 million; that's a whopping 5 per cent of the population. Sugar is everywhere. It shows up in breads, yoghurt, peanut butter and sauces.

Ironically, back in the 1970s the Americans decided there was too much unhealthy fat in the food being produced so they took it out. Unfortunately, if you take the fats out of food it tastes like cardboard; so they replaced it with sugar.

Although it may be scientifically inaccurate to say that sugar is a poison, it certainly acts like one. It damages organs, it interferes with brain signals and it promotes addictive behaviour.

Go to your kitchen cupboard and take a look at the amounts of sugar in the pre-prepared food you eat. Ready meals are often astonishing: sugar is everywhere.

To get more balance in your energy and to keep your spacesuit bright and shiny, check how much refined sugar you're consuming. If you cut your sugar intake you will feel much better, be able to connect more easily to your true self and look mighty fine on that beach.

As there is nothing sweet in nature that is poisonous, our subconscious associates sweet with safe. It's amazing what you can hide with a little sugar.

Sweet ain't safe no longer. Sweet should make you suspicious.

SLEEP AND REST

Sleep deprivation costs US companies $63.2 billion per year, according to the National Sleep Foundation. Fifty million Americans suffer from sleep problems, many stemming from the long work hours and stress and, yes, much too much coffee.

This deprivation, as any parent of young children will know, results in living in a weird, altered reality. It affects your mood, your relationships and your ability to concentrate.

In Britain, 45 per cent of the working population sleep less than seven hours a night. There is a very close link between depression and poor sleep. To have a healthy relationship with your work, you need to get enough zzzzzzzz's.

Some very simple things can help you with that. First, ensure your room is dark, cool and quiet. Endeavour to go to bed at the same time each night. Avoid looking at screens for an hour before you sleep. Read a book in bed, as it is a proven relaxant. Mobile phones should not be in the bedroom, full stop. And a little passion can also help bring on the dreams (well, it can for men; women tend to lie awake afterwards, swearing under their breath).

Most importantly for a good night's sleep, do not work late into the evenings. Work will stimulate your mind and make it increasingly difficult for you to journey off to the land of Nod.

To help ourselves recuperate from a hard day's work, we must

LEAVE
YOUR WORK
AT WORK

also make the most of our downtime; we have to leave work alone. All too often we are still thinking about work and sending the occasional email into the evening. This makes it particularly tough to switch off. By doing so, we dilute the quality of rest that we have and we damage the attention we give to our loved ones.

By continuing to work at night we increase our stress levels, which in turn puts us at greater risk of cardiovascular disease and depression, not to mention the threat it poses to our relationships.

If you have to work out of office hours then go somewhere other than your living room and close the door. Having a physical boundary helps keep our relationship with our work healthy.

But ask yourself: what is more important now? Another email, or my health and my family?

So if you can, turn off your email when you arrive home – and leave your work at work.

BOOZE

This piece is going to amuse the hell out of anybody who has ever been on a night out with me, for eight years in the brewing industry has led me to enjoy a little refreshment on occasion. But maybe with a little more maturity I am starting to understand the dangers of mixing booze and business. I don't mean the dangers of getting thoroughly pissed at the Christmas party and telling your boss what you really think of them, but rather the insidious nature of pressure drinking.

I know how much pressure we can be under to drink when we ordinarily would not. When we are young and less confident it is hard to say no, and as social currency is part of how we get on in work, it's important for us not to appear as a killjoy. A study undertaken by the Reason Foundation found that men who don't drink are paid 13 per cent less than those who do; more alarmingly, for women it's 26 per cent. So the pressure is on.

Some people are born to sup pints of ale or glasses of rosé after work and it has little effect upon their health, energy or relationships. Others are not so lucky. If you are one of those, be the grown-up and steer clear.

It's important to still be social, so of course you should go to the pub on occasion, but give the shots of Jägermeister a wide berth.

If booze isn't your thing, think how you can achieve social currency without it. You could organize a softball league, some tickets to a gig, a sushi course or a bit of Bollywood dancing. Make the event rich and stimulating so alcohol is no longer the singular focus and people will thank you for it. Trust me, you won't be the only one who wants to avoid unnecessary drinking.

Too much booze will eventually deplete your energy and will make it tougher for you to shine as brightly as you can. Keep a close eye on how much you drink because it can soon become one of the hardest addictions to break. Whatever your poison, knowing your limits isn't just about not having one too many, it's about maintaining your energy in the long run.

DOWNTIME

I often work with leadership teams when they are away from the office. More often than not, participants have travelled from all around the globe to be there, and are in various states of jet-lagged confusion. It always amazes me how, when these groups come together, they are immediately forced into having 'fun' when really they ought to be in bed so they can be on top form the next day.

Social time is important for building relationships, but we are not machines. We need some downtime to get our energy back and we certainly don't need the pressure of three-hour dinners if we are to be free.

If you have flown through time zones to a conference and have spent all day working flat out with your colleagues and you're then encouraged to socialize over dinner, feel free to decline. Whoever organizes these events clearly never has to experience them. They are hell.

It's bad enough that you're working away from home and have to share the same hotel as your colleagues; you certainly don't have to eat with them as well – it's not a legal requirement. Swim, run, shop, relax, go to bed . . . and then come back pumped tomorrow. Of course, if you don't get together too often and a big night out is a treat, then fill your boots. But only if you want to.

One of my clients arranges regular fortnightly visits by their leadership team to their markets. The unfortunate team members are working from the moment they wake up until they sleep, over breakfast, lunch and dinner. They come back wrecked and both they and their partners dread it. What is that achieving?

Business trips can be amazingly rewarding and productive if properly planned, but don't make them torture. If you are a party animal and need a couple of tequilas before every dinner, that's your shout – just don't bully others to do the same. Give people space.

BODY WISDOM

There is no freedom without awareness. If we are blind to who we are and what's happening to us, we could be trapped in no end of mental prisons without the slightest clue why.

To flip metaphors, without awareness we are like a small boat on the ocean that has become rudderless and lost its sail. Our only choice is to drift with the current and be battered by the winds and the storms; helpless and easily pushed around.

The greater our sense of awareness, the greater our choice. The greater our choice, the more chance we have to choose the type of freedom we want, and not one that has been designed for us. To become aware we need to be more sensitized to ourselves and our energy, which is one of the reasons I have been banging on about the dangers of working too hard, drinking too much coffee, filling ourselves with refined sugar, distracting ourselves with technology and then washing it down with a gallon of Chablis.

All of these things desensitize us and keep us numb to the messages that we should be listening out for. For some people, tuning in to energetic connections to your true self can be a struggle. It's something we all need to practise every day.

However, we are blessed with having an incredibly easy-to-read dashboard that can tell us accurately how our engine is running. That dashboard is our body. Our bodies are amazing things. They are designed to last a lifetime (boom boom) and if they are properly maintained will facilitate an amazing journey.

They also tell us when things aren't quite right. They give us clues as to when our mental, emotional and spiritual energies are unsynchronized and in need of realignment. Many of the ailments that we feel physically are mere representations of these energies being out of kilter. If we spot those instances more readily we can often head off a couple of days in bed by dealing with the cause instead of the physical symptom.

Dr Robert V. Gerard, psychologist and healer, believes that over 75 per cent of all visits to medical agencies could be eliminated if each individual became accountable for his or her own treatment and healing. I believe that's true, but for the healing to work we need to understand what is driving the disease.

A few months ago I woke up feeling terrible. My whole body ached and I felt exhausted. My head was foggy and I found it impossible to concentrate on anything. Even breakfast with my wife and kids left me feeling more tired, not my usual exhilarated and playful self. I had some pressing work to do, so I spent a few hours on it, struggling through the haze of what was turning into proper full-blown flu.

By late morning the aches and pains had grown so bad that I could barely turn my head to the side. All I could think about was going to bed, pulling the duvet over my head and signing off from the world. I had a Skype call scheduled with my personal coach, David, but I was preparing to cancel. Man, I was feeling sorry for myself: coaching sounded painful.

What I wanted was an ally who would figuratively put his arm round me and say, 'There, there. Isn't it tough being you? You go sleep for a few days and I'll look after everything else in your life.' But it wasn't to be. David isn't the kind who lets you cry off easily. He knows that if I am feeling bad, there is usually something deeper going on. So there wasn't a hope he would let me off the hook.

First, he helped me get my head back on track with some breathing. Once I had regained some perspective he asked me what beliefs I was holding that were making me feel like death warmed up. It was a clever question and it took me a while to answer.

The first things that came into my head had no power or resonance; they were the obvious things, such as that I had a lot of travel coming up and I hadn't been home very much recently and that I had a pile of admin to work through, blah blah blah.

Then something popped into my head that I hadn't been expecting. We had just completed some work with a client and it had achieved some great results; they now wanted us to do a big global deal. This meant sitting down to plan a proper programme and scheduling dates and resources and getting into all the nitty-gritty detail that makes business work. The clients also wanted to make sure that, as they were spending millions of dollars, they were getting real value, too.

I talked a little about this and David noticed that my energy had dropped and my breathing had become jammed. After some gentle probing it became obvious that I was thinking it was all a bit too much like hard work and there was no fun to be had.

I had become a petulant child.

It's such a lot of work.

There's so many details to be sorted out.

This will consume the next six months of my life.

So much could go wrong.

Not only do they want me to do all this work, I bet they'll want a discount and we never discount, so I'm going to have a tough conversation.

These negatives swirling round my head had poisoned my energy system, so my dashboard (my body) was letting me know. My body was coughing and spluttering and giving me a proper dose of man flu.

David and I then explored the facts of the matter:

My business was very successful.

I had just landed one of the sexiest pieces of work of my life.

My partners were born to do this work and are the best on the planet at doing it, so I had a great team for support.

This job meant we wouldn't have to worry about income for a good while.

It could be the one that made us famous and helped us change the world, or at least our world.

With any luck I'd be going to Japan, one of the few countries I'd never travelled to and couldn't wait to visit.

As soon as I started to talk about these positives the most amazing thing happened. The aches disappeared. I could now turn my head without my neck knotting up. The fogginess faded. At the start of the session, a whole ten minutes ago, I'd felt utterly exhausted, so much so that I could barely stay awake; but now I felt energized, refreshed and gagging to get out in the world. I had become free.

You need to check in with your body at regular intervals. Set your phone to vibrate every twenty minutes in your pocket. Whenever it does so, take a big deep breath and notice how you are feeling. If you do this for a week your conscious awareness will grow enormously and you will no longer need the phone.

(And if your phone doesn't work like that, you could always download the free Upping Your Elvis app . . .)

Take a deep breath right now and, as you do so, stretch your spine upwards. As you keep breathing in a relaxed way, notice how your body feels.

Are there any aches or pains that don't really belong? What is the quality of your mental energy like? Is it clear and focused and open to opportunity, or does it feel sluggish, distracted, fixated or a bit hazy? What is the sense of connection like to yourself and what you're doing? What feelings are you experiencing?

By checking in regularly as to how you are feeling you will start to become more aware when things aren't right. When you notice that things aren't quite right, ask yourself the question: 'What beliefs am I holding right now that aren't serving me?' You'll know which ones they are because when you find them they will resonate. When you have spotted them, turn them round by asking yourself: 'What are the real facts about that?'

By focusing on the truth, we can liberate ourselves from our natural tendency to fear the worst, and be free to have a better day full of impact and fun. Not to mention fewer days feeling sorry for ourselves, sniffling in bed.

I recently noticed that I seemed to have little energy, everything seemed hard and my wife mentioned I wasn't smiling much. When I looked at my beliefs, I realized that I was feeling very responsible for my work, my business, my people, my family, my home etc. etc., and felt all the pressure was on me.

When I turned it round and remembered that I had a fabulous team helping me with all of this and that we always do better together, my whole energy shifted and I regained the usual spring in my step.

POWER UP

If your overall energy is jammed it shows up in your body, but equally if you get your body right it helps your energy. Everything is linked and therefore your mojo can be improved by simply getting your body feeling great.

Amy Cuddy, a social scientist at Harvard Business School, delivered a classic TED Talk explaining that if we adopt more powerful poses it has a proven impact on the way we perform.

Just by sitting in a more powerful way – back straight and leaning forward, shoulders back and head up – you are up to 26 per cent more likely to take a risk. These poses increase our testosterone levels while decreasing our cortisol levels, a hormone that is related to stress. Just holding the pose for two minutes can make a world of difference to how we feel and how we perform.

I often see people who are crushed by their work taking very submissive poses. They are hunched, head down, and looking small. In these positions you can't even breathe properly, let alone get the energy flowing. If you deliberately get your body feeling good by stretching out and holding a pose, it will give you more perspective and make it easier for you to feel free.

Liberate your body and your mind will follow

HOW ARE YOU NOW?

Stop and notice how you are now.

How would you describe your energy?

Notice that there is a busyness in your head and there are some tensions in your body.

Breathe into those and relax.

When you remember who you really are, these lumps and bumps and worries melt away.

Breathe and slow it all down. Remember that your true essence is perfect and that everything is just how it should be.

Sit quietly and chill; let everything wash over you.

When you remember who you are, you don't need to fight, as all is in balance.

We may be
in a serious
business,
but we don't
have to take
it seriously.

PLAY

When business is taken too seriously, it's a hard trap to escape. There are some organizations where, when you walk into reception, the energy is overwhelmingly uptight. People are running around being very busy, wearing fantastic designer clothes, and nobody is smiling or laughing. It's a very serious business.

I feel like running and screaming to escape the pretence that we are all so perfect, clever and important. Work is about life and a big part of life is about having fun. If we take things too seriously, we get locked into using only our conscious thinking and have little or no access to our creative genius.

Not only do we handicap ourselves, but then we spread this restriction to anyone else we deal with. Yet no one wants to work in a grumpy place where the weight of the world is on everyone's shoulders. It's miserable. It feels as if the hope has been sucked out of every meeting room and that the only way to win is by working harder and sweating more. Well, you can forget that.

To be amazing and to be free we need to play more. I regularly encounter leaders who feel they are responsible for everything. They believe that if they run a meeting and it doesn't go well, it's all their fault. They believe that if the company isn't coming up with constant new innovations, it's all down to them. They believe that if their people lack motivation and energy, they must be a poor leader. That simply can't be true.

It's nice when leaders take responsibility and own the company's performance, but that responsibility has to be shared. Organizations are complicated and have many working parts. Anyone trying to control all aspects of them will die in a state of lunacy, with a massive Scotch habit and few friends.

Yes, we should be ambitious and turn up ready to create real impact. But for us to truly unleash our brilliance we must then ignore what happens after we have lit the touchpaper and instead focus on making ourselves as shiny as we can possibly be. By doing so we will lighten the mood not only of ourselves but also of those around us, and thus encourage others to play a bit more too.

'Play is the highest form of research.'

Albert Einstein

If we take work too seriously we will never do anything new. Those who are too serious believe that everything needs to be measured. But how can you measure creativity, energy, commitment, excitement, confidence or humour? All these things will set your organization, department or team apart from the rest.

Play is all about newness and experimentation, and by playing we can access more of our creative genius. By being more playful we create more energy, which in turn attracts people to us. We want to be attractive in business so that we make people want to help us and share their talent and ideas. This makes us freer to do amazing work as we have increased our resources just by being more fun.

Even the very erudite *Harvard Business Review*, a journal with vast research credentials and which employs some of the finest brains on this planet, found that 'managers with a sense of humour were viewed more favourably'. Who'd have thought?

Stress is one of the most common causes of long-term

sickness – it costs the UK economy around £8.4 billion every year, according to the Chartered Institute of Personnel and Development (cipd.co.uk). A study of over 2,500 employees found that 93 per cent believed laughter helped them reduce their stress levels. (I'm guessing the other 7 per cent worked in legal departments.)

Groupon is an internet-based business that made its fortune offering discounted daily deals. When founder Andrew Mason was axed by the board after an $80 million loss over three months, he emailed the people of Groupon:

I've decided that I'd like to spend more time with my family. Just kidding – I was fired today. If you're wondering why . . . you haven't been paying attention. I'm OK with having failed at this part of the journey. If Groupon was Battletoads it would be like I made it all the way to the Terra Tubes without dying on my first ever play through.

Battletoads was an impossibly hard Nintendo game. What I love about this email is that it's playful and his personality runs through it. He managed to flex his perspective and make what could be a rather painful situation more celebratory. It's certainly not the goodbye statement that most senior executives would write.

Being playful by injecting some humour helps us keep perspective when it gets tricky, and means our workplace is somewhere we want to be. A friend and client of mine, Simon Daglish, is a bit of an adventurer. He likes nothing more than to trek across continents of snow for a good cause. He was recently in Iceland training twenty wounded servicemen from around the world for an unsupported attempt on the South Pole. He told me:

We were up on a glacier in the north of the island. It was minus twenty degrees Centigrade and blowing fifty knots. The conditions were atrocious.

Most of the team had lost one limb or another [on active service]. One of the team had had both his eyes blown out and was completely blind. He'd had a dreadful day, constantly being knocked over by the wind or tripping over his skis. He'd never skied before. At the end of the day we made the decision to come off the glacier and were picked up by some Arctic trucks.

Once everyone was safely inside the truck, the driver who had picked us up said, 'At least I got you back in one piece.' The blind man, as quick as a flash, with a mischievous grin on his face said, 'Can't you see most of us have lost one piece or another. Are you fucking blind?'

Genius. If I am ever frostbitten and exhausted, I want that man with me.

The fear of getting things wrong keeps us small and trapped. If everything has to work we will never do anything new. Risk is implicit in business and it's what makes it interesting. If you never take a risk, your business will die. I am a believer in taking lots of little risks every day in the form of playful experiments. If we mess with the rules regularly, we get better and better at learning from those experiments. If we just save experimenting for special occasions, we are going to be useless at it.

Bill Hewlett, co-founder of Hewlett-Packard, really believes in what he calls 'small-bet innovation'. He found that HP needed to make a hundred small bets to find six breakthroughs.

Have a think about what you can do today.

What playful experiment might deliver a bit of genius?

Loving Your Caveman

5

THE PREHISTORIC
BRAIN

The pace of change in technology, society and innovation has accelerated in the last fifty years. For the most part our lives are being run by concepts that are less than ten years old – just think of smartphones and the apps they run.

Despite this pace, we haven't changed at all. We are very similar now to how we have been for the last 50,000 years, both physically and mentally. This means our brains are still essentially prehistoric, and badly designed for many of today's challenges and the world in which we live. They are best suited to scanning our environment for danger, finding food and fighting off sabre-toothed tigers. Our brains have an inbuilt 'negativity bias' which conditions us instinctively to fight or flee or freeze, depending on which will maximize our chances of survival.

So our brains are constantly looking for bad news. When they find it, they create strong emotional and physical reactions and plumb them straight into our memory as a powerful anchor in case we experience it again.

This was a great blueprint for survival. Even today, were I to come face to face with a sabre-toothed tiger, I'd know instantly what to do from my past experience; I wouldn't have to think about it at all. Our bodies respond to visuals in thirty-three milliseconds – far faster than we can consciously comprehend – so we are subconsciously driven. If we see things we don't like, our reactions are instant and instinctive and animalistic.

Although such threats no longer exist, our brains are still looking for them, and in the absence of real dangers, we often imagine them and react to what isn't even there. Think about how many times you have worried about something that has never happened. What was once key to survival is now a handicap to being free. We are ruled by our fears and slaves to our imaginations.

As Dan Gardner explains in his book *The Science of Fear*,

> *When it comes to the evolution of psychology, we should imagine the development of the human brain by equating the past 2 million years of human development to a 201-page book. Of that book, 200 pages would cover the entire time our species spent being nomadic hunter-gatherers in the Stone Age. The last page would cover our time as an agrarian society. The last paragraphs on the final page would cover the last two centuries of the world we now live in. We are cavemen.*

The effect of possessing such an ancient design of brain is that we spend much of our time in a reactive mode that is triggered by external stimuli. This reactive mode has been likened to an inner homelessness. We can feel disconnected, unappreciated, unloved, even unseen. It's a mode in which it's hard to connect with others and be empathetic, compassionate and kind.

It's a place where we do not feel free because the state we are in is not one we have chosen. Instead it's a reactive one, with a hair trigger. It's a place that is driven by fear, and by definition that removes us from consciousness and the ability to find perspectives that make us feel good, expansive and shiny. Just think for a moment about times that you have misinterpreted an innocent situation as a threat.

Misreading emails is a classic example. Language is so open to interpretation that often our prehistoric brains see a negative when actually a positive is intended. I am sure you have seen ferocious keyboard wars break out for no reason at all. When have you overreacted because your prehistoric brain has sensed danger and sent you out of the cave fighting?

To overcome this hair trigger, we need to take hold of ourselves again by slowing everything down.

When we react to a threat, our heart rate soars and our minds start to race. This is brilliant for fighting, as it produces lots of adrenaline and a sharp focus. The problem is that we then find it impossible to see other perspectives. So first we must slow everything down by breathing deeply and smiling. This helps us break away from the fight response. Then we need to find the whole thing funny; if we can laugh at our situation, our irrational anger will weaken.

Then we can try to see the situation from a different perspective. If it's an email that has got you riled, think about the possible intention behind it. How would your partner read it? My wife, who is German, often interprets things differently from me, which can be a useful frame to free me up. If she or I get stuck with a negative reaction, we help each other by trading some different perspectives.

As you practise this, the cave-dweller becomes a friend instead of a handicap, providing an energy boost without forcing you into a full-on wrestling match.

FEAR

Fear is useful. It stops us doing stupid things. Without fear we would have tigers as pets and we would juggle chainsaws for giggles. That might not work out so well for some.

Fear, however, is one of the biggest traps that we will face in business. Fear will make us become someone else, it will take away our shine and it will make life no fun at all – if we let it.

Sir Ben Kingsley, one of Britain's greatest actors, often used to sit on set even when his character was not involved. This is unusual as most actors go to relax in their trailers and use such breaks as downtime. When asked why he was watching the scenes he explained that he wanted to be around in case people realized that he wasn't that good and was being overpaid.

Whether he was joking or not, it is true that we all have fears. It's part of the human condition. The question is, are they useful?

We live in a more fearful society than ever. The media love to feed off this fear, and politicians know they would have little control over the population without it. If it weren't for the Falklands war would Margaret Thatcher have been prime minister for over a decade? If it weren't for the Axis of Evil would anyone ever have listened to George W. Bush?

People are manipulated using fear and I'm afraid that it's starting to mess with our psyche.

The summer of 2001 was notoriously branded 'The summer

Our self-worth should never be dictated to by other people's opinions.

of the shark' by *Time* magazine. There were seventy-nine unprovoked shark attacks globally and the media went crazy. They told tragic stories of children being eaten and surfers being ripped apart. The reporting was incredibly vivid and scared everyone out of the water, as the public came to believe that the seas were shark infested and extremely dangerous.

The truth was, nothing had changed.

Every year there are about a hundred shark attacks. In New York alone you are ten times more likely to be bitten by a human than bitten by a shark anywhere in the world.

In the same year 115 people died every day in car accidents, but that didn't make the news or stop people driving.

The media play us like puppets and we love to dance for them. We are scared of being too fat, too thin, too smart, too dumb, no fun, too shallow, broke, rich, busy, quiet, pale, tanned, short, tall, old, young . . .

It's our obsession. Our prehistoric brains, always on the lookout for danger, don't take a great deal of coaxing into a fearful place. If a magazine can create palpitations because we realize we don't have the latest frock, then the real and visceral experience of our workplace can have us flipping out every day of the week.

We all need to have external validation to reinforce our self-identity, but its influence is hugely disproportionate.

If we spend our time worrying about what other people think, we will never get round to living our own lives. At work the perception of what we stand for and what we are good at becomes career currency. We try to be aware that our brand exists and we need to make sure we are accentuating the bits that we love.

Our self-worth should never be dictated by other people's opinions. We cannot live our lives for anyone else. We have to do what is true to us and then let go.

We cannot fully predict how people will react to what we do, what we say, how we dress or how we talk. The beauty and weirdness of people is such that we will continually be surprised by others' reactions. That's what makes life exciting and sometimes bizarre. There is no point trying to please everyone, because we can only fail.

As long as you are living up to your values, with good intent and in a way that you believe is positive, then you can do no more.

Here's a brief checklist to refer to if you're ever worried about which action to choose:

WHAT WOULD YOU DO IF YOU KNEW YOU COULDN'T FAIL?

IS THIS AN ACTION YOU WOULD DEFEND AND BE HAPPY TO EXPLAIN TO YOUR PARENTS?

IS IT MAKING THE WORLD A BETTER PLACE?

WHEN YOU THINK ABOUT IT CALMLY, DOES IT FEEL LIKE THE RIGHT THING TO DO?

DOES IT MAKE YOU A BETTER PERSON?

WILL SOMEONE ELSE'S LIFE BE ENRICHED AS A RESULT?

If what you're planning ticks a lot of boxes, then do it.

Be yourself, stand proud and true and tall. If others don't like it, love them anyway.

PARANOIA IS OUT TO GET YOU!

Paranoia increases in urban environments. There is twice the level of psychosis in metropolitan than in rural areas. More people and more interaction means more misinterpretation of intentions.

Some business environments can feel like small cities. It's no wonder that 40 per cent of employees believe that 'their colleagues are talking behind their back' and that 10 per cent of them believe 'someone has got it in for them', according to Professor Daniel Freeman of King's College London.

If you couple this natural tendency to worry too much about how people feel about you with the rise of social networking, it's easy to see why people are becoming more sensitized to the voices in their heads. Facebook paranoia is a very real phenomenon that breeds self-doubt and shaky self-esteem.

> 'People who use [social media] sites are aware that people are talking about each other all the time, so it would be natural to assume that they are talking about you too.'

Philip Corr, Professor of Psychology

> '**Relax. You're not paranoid. I really am slagging you off behind your back.**'
>
> Ricky Gervais on Twitter

As many as 70 per cent of successful people experience feelings of being a phoney (a statistic cited in *The Impostor Phenomenon* by Pauline Rose Clance). The fear of being found out is prevalent in all walks of business, and has most recently been linked to high achievers.

The principle here is simple: if you believe you're about to be found out, you work much harder. When you do get success, you attribute it to the hard work and not to your natural talents. Therefore you keep working harder, bringing success through more sweat and toil than is perhaps necessary. I have worked with many talented people who were driven by the belief that they might be found out at any second. Such people work hard, but their energy is out of control and they often burn out.

It's a dangerous, exhausting cycle.

Professor Karl Aquino from the University of British Columbia's Sauder School of Business believes that workplace paranoia can only lead to negativity. 'It's perfectly natural for people to wonder how others view them, especially when social acceptance in the workplace is often rewarded with power and financial compensation,' he says. 'However, our research shows employees should do their best to keep their interactions positive and ignore the negative.'

This makes perfect sense when you pull it apart. If you search for evidence that people don't like you, that is exactly what you'll find. Our brains will help us to collect whatever evidence we ask them to: if you look for shit, that's what you'll find. Equally, if you spread positivity, compassion and love you will receive much of it back.

Paranoia is fuelled by the belief that we are separate, discrete personalities that are in some way all in competition. When we remember our true essence is not the experience we are enjoying but a higher energetic self, we no longer worry about what people think, or indeed what drives those thoughts.

When you breathe well and smile, all the paranoia and politics become water off a duck's back. When you are truly connected, every day feels just right.

Think about something that is annoying or frustrating you right now.

Notice the emotion it creates in you.

Now play with it.

Breathe deep, sit straight and smile.

What other perspectives could you take that would give you more power, more fun, help you move forward and be excited?

How can you find something valuable in the situation?

What lessons may be available to you?

How can it make you feel thankful?

Is there some compassion this moment can tap?

What about it is downright funny?

Keep playing with the problem until you feel free from irritation; then you'll have the confidence that you can free yourself from any negative feeling, if you decide to do so.

THE CRITIC

With social networking and 24/7 communication, there have never been so many critics on this planet. I can understand the desire to share opinion, and opinion can certainly be useful where it is seen as positive stimulus. But I find it extraordinary that one critic's opinion should shape someone's future behaviour.

The people who create value are not the people commenting, they are the people doing. They are not the ones who spectate from the sidelines but the ones who fall over and scrape their knees, mess things up and still carry on.

Do not be scared of the critic.

Yes, what they say may hurt and the language they use might be designed to injure; but remember, critics don't change anything. They don't create anything. All they do is trade in negativity and therefore spend their whole lives seeing it. They are parasites who feed off brave people's actions, nothing more.

I feel sorry for them. The nature of selective attention is such that if you seek to see the bad around you, and are forever asking why things don't work and why they are crap, before long that is all you can see. I know that critics provide the occasional glowing review as well, but positivity doesn't sell papers, attract audiences or create more buzz. It's sad, but that's the reality.

Most critics live a monochrome life in which the highs have

DO NOT
BE SCARED OF
THE CRITIC

been dampened and the only real emotional kicks they get are from the lows. It's tough being a critic, living in a place where the sunshine is never quite warm enough.

There are, in my view, two types of critic. The first are those who are brave enough to say, 'That's shit,' proudly and loudly, and look you in the eye as they do so. I have some admiration for them as they are happy to stand by what they believe in. These are easy to deal with: once they have shared their opinion you can then ask them how you can do things better. In creative sessions, if someone keeps judging the ideas that are put forward and saying they won't work, I often ask them, 'Well, tell me how it *could* work, then.' Immediately they have to put up or shut up: either help and own the problem, or stop rubbishing the ideas.

More sinister is the shifty critic; the one who whispers in people's ears but never tells you to your face. It's cynical, poisonous behaviour. Cynicism is not bad per se; as long as it is voiced, it can be dealt with. But negative corridor chats – about someone but not in front of them – are something that must be dealt with. If you can't say something to someone's face and are not prepared to deal with the consequences and are not committed to improve things as a result, suck it up and hold it in. The world will thank you for it.

If you think that people are doing this to you, confront them in the nicest way; share your thoughts and ask for theirs. Get the moose on the table and have a proper chat (see page 93 on how to do that).

Next time you are concerned about somebody's opinion or criticism, first run the rule over your own actions. Make sure that you believe in yourself and in what you're doing. If you do, then you are free: free to self-express, be yourself and lead an extraordinary work life.

If what you do does raise a critic's hackles, don't become

defensive or feel wounded. Send them some love and play with your perspectives until you can appreciate theirs. There is always some value to be gained by seeing things through another pair of eyes, even jaundiced ones. It's imperative to remember that no criticism can make you bad, wrong, small or silly. It's purely a judgement, one person's opinion and nothing more.

Many people decide that it is safer to hide away so as not to draw critics' attention. They make themselves small as a means of protection.

One chap I came across, who is very bright and successful, used to joke that the only way to survive was to be a 'corporate cockroach' – he said that such employees were almost invisible and impossible to kill. For many, unfortunately, this isn't a joke: it's a daily reality.

In that regard, I slightly regret the choice of subtitle for my last book *SHINE: How to Survive and Thrive at Work*. It sounded good, and the 'thriving' part is fine, but surviving is not what business is about.

Love the Unlovable

This one is a favourite from my good buddy and co-conspirator, David Pearl.

I would like you to imagine something that you would never let into your house, something that offends your taste entirely. It could be one of those dolls with a knitted dress that so elegantly sits over a spare toilet roll, or a poster that tells you to keep calm and carry on . . . Anything that makes you squirm.

Now that you have chosen something that you find suitably vulgar, you need to learn to love it.

By playing with your perspectives, find a way to appreciate that object. It can't be completely without merit: thousands of people have chosen to buy it, after all. It's purely a matter of taste. Beauty really is in the eye of the beholder; play with your eye until you love it!

By practising on something unimportant, you will soon appreciate how easy it is to find the beauty in everything and everyone.

This is a foundational skill in not being judgemental and making every day a shiny one.

We all have amazing gifts and everyone has their own unique way of creating value in this world. If we don't live up to that every day, we are denying this planet the brilliance that it so desperately needs, and we are denying ourselves the full human experience that we are on this earth to enjoy.

Stand up and shine with freedom.

PLAY NICELY, DON'T TELL FIBS

A simple way to reduce your fears and worries is to always play nicely and never tell fibs.

Never do anything that you don't want anyone else to know about. Because these days, someone will. Everything is becoming more transparent and therefore hiding mistakes is becoming trickier. It's much better to fess up and move on.

Even better is to make sure that everything you do is how you want to be remembered. We are often given opportunities to do things that are off-brand. Don't take them.

I was once travelling to Hong Kong on business with a colleague in my former agency. It was an overnight flight from London and the airport was rammed. At check-in we were each offered £2,000 in cash to downgrade to economy – business class was overbooked. Now, that much cash is always nice, but it's also dangerous. Our clients had paid for us to travel business class because that's what we needed to get rest and be on tip-top form to deliver their work. We would be, in effect, stealing from them.

If I were to have taken the deal, I would have spent months worrying that someone would find out, and that my lack of integrity would be my downfall. It was so much easier to just say no and never have to think about it again. By doing so, my head was clear and no guilt could follow me. What a relief!

If you always play nicely, there will be no repercussions for your actions. Nobody's nose will be out of joint, no vendettas will come your way, your conscience will be clean and there will be no reason to fret. If you always tell the truth, you never have to worry about remembering the lies you told or be concerned about being found out. Playing it straight takes the stress out of work.

You can never guarantee how people will respond to you. This is one of the joys of being alive. Everybody sees you in their own unique and special way and therefore will have their own unique and special views of you. You cannot control those views and nor should you try. However, if you live life by your values and act in a way that you will not regret, regardless of how you are viewed, you will be true to yourself. That is all that matters.

That doesn't mean to say you can be insensitive or malicious by absolving yourself from the effects of your actions. But it does mean that if those actions are led by your heart and with honourable intent, then what other people think is irrelevant. (That said, most people will think you're pretty special, which is nice.)

PENGUIN OR CUCKOO?

In nature, animals spend far more time cooperating than fighting. Vampire bats share food with those of their kin who are malnourished, while penguins group together for warmth. Some birds will team up to protect themselves from attack. Being nice is a big part of normal behaviour for many species.

There are, however, some species that play rough. Sharks that eat their siblings while still in the womb or the cuckoos that throw their adopted brothers and sisters out of their nests so they get the food they need to grow. Do you want to be a penguin or a cuckoo?

If you rise to power through manipulation and deception, you will always be in fear that others will do the same to you. It's tempting at times to play the villain, to beat your competition, to just win. That edge we gain through our drive to succeed is useful – but don't do it at the cost of others.

Everyone wants to be the hero. Promotions are limited, salary rises are competitive, budgets are finite and to be fought for. But you can do that simply by being good; you don't have to kill the competition. When we get into that mode, the prehistoric brain kicks in. It's designed for fighting and therefore makes us act in a responsive and unconscious way. We lose the feel for possibility and end up doing our work less well.

Chill out, smile and realize that it's just a game. We can all win together. Business brings out the dark side in people all too often: buck the trend and be a shining light. Play nicely, and the chances are that others will too. (And if they don't, perhaps this isn't the culture that you want to work in.)

UNEMPLOYABLE

I have been unemployable for a long time. My earliest bosses found me a struggle to manage and as time has gone on I have become even more confirmed in my behaviours and attitudes. I am unemployable.

That's fine, because now I have tasted the freedom of running my own business I would find it a challenge to work for anyone else again.

Setting up your own business can appear intimidating and yet it's one of the most liberating things you can do. We often believe it carries a far higher risk than it actually does. I find there is more security having my own business than being employed. When you're employed you can be sacked; when you have your own business you cannot. When you're employed you have a fixed income; when you have your own business you can aim to turn it up or turn it down, depending on what your needs are.

This planet is run by small businesses: 96 per cent of all UK businesses employ fewer than ten people. Over the last five years the number of businesses employing one or two people has exploded by more than 50 per cent to over 400,000. These companies have proven to be amazingly robust during the economic downturn, suffering the lowest insolvency rate and achieving the second healthiest financial score compared to other types of business.

The truth is, setting up your own small business is not that risky at all. Relative to other business sectors, micro enterprises provide more new jobs, more innovation and creativity, do more for their communities, and make their employees happier.

Running your own show has a different energy about it, because you are ultimately responsible for your income. Of course, if you are among those who worry too much, you may find that a burden. Self-employment is not for everybody, but the freedom that comes with it is extraordinary. I wish I had struck out on my own earlier in my life.

HIT REFRESH

Over the course of our lives, we start to get trapped by our vision of the world. The things we fail to question every day start to seem natural, true. The world becomes fixed.

'Everything we hear is an opinion, not a fact. Everything we see is a perspective, not the truth.'

Marcus Aurelius, Roman emperor

We start to believe that we really are Jed Bowerman in sales, who has a rather average life laid out that involves mortgages, children, some rather nice holidays and a stag do that is still talked about with quiet reverence.

We start to believe that although we have some control over our lives, our ability to shake things up is restricted by some well-defined parameters. Our beliefs about who we are, the world we live in and what's important shape every aspect of our actions.

We have to practise regularly challenging those beliefs to make sure they are not restricting us and taking away our freedom without our realizing it. If we start to accept our conceptions of the world as fact rather than opinion, we'll never progress.

> **'The belief that one's own view of reality is the only reality is the most dangerous of all delusions.'**
>
> Paul Watzlawick, family therapist

Fyodor Dostoevsky was a gloomy and paranoid young man. He was sensitive and struggled to see the brilliance in life. In 1849 he was arrested with a group of friends known as the Petrashevsky Circle, who opposed Tsarist rule. Considered revolutionaries, they were sentenced to death by firing squad.

While standing in front of the guns, he considered his life past and present and future. Just before the triggers were pulled and his brief existence was drawn to a close, a messenger rode up with a pardon. Although he was instead sentenced to hard labour in Siberia, that moment had a profound impact on the rest of his life:

When I look back on my past and think how much time I wasted on nothing, and how much time has been lost in futilities, errors, laziness, incapacity to live; how little I appreciate it . . .

Life is a gift, life is happiness, and every minute can be an eternal happiness . . .

Life is everywhere, life is in ourselves, not in the exterior.

WHAT WOULD
BE YOUR
WAKE-UP CALL?

This vision was created through an extreme crisis that almost literally brought Dostoevsky back from the dead.

What would be your wake-up call? What would it take for you to reset your beliefs about who you are and your perceptions about this life, to make sure that you never squandered another second?

Think about it.

Close your eyes and breathe into that question. It could be the biggest question you ever ask.

Any moment that provokes us to question our reality has the potential to change us. These moments can shift our consciousness and help us remember who we truly want to be and what is important to us.

In terms of our overall existence as a species, it was only yesterday that we all believed that Earth was the centre of the solar system, and that matter was solid.

Beliefs are purely perception and are transient.

I can't wait for the spaceships to land so all those clever folk out there who think they know the answer to everything will have to think again.

Tee hee.

(NOT) LOSING THE PLOT

Not so long ago I got really cross.

The trigger was an email from somebody who had hired me for a speaking event. I live three hours from London and I had been needed at the venue by 9 a.m., so I had come up the night before to stay in Town. When I invoiced my fee and expenses for my hotel and train, my client responded by telling me that he would pay reasonable expenses but in his view these were not reasonable and therefore I had been unethical by incurring them.

I lost the plot. My mind was racing and making no end of judgements about him, his business and the comments that he'd made. I was so out-of-state that I was useless. I had gone into fight-or-flight mode, and quite frankly I fancied a fight.

This type of reaction is common when we feel wronged or unfairly dealt with. Our judgements kick in and before long we have lost all perspective of what is important.

Fortunately, being the emotional ninja that I am, I noticed that something was going on and stopped. Unless I got my perspective back I would be stuck in this emotional state, feeling grumpy and hard done by. I find that the fastest way for me to regain that perspective is to sit straight and breathe deep and smile and remember who I really am.

So that's what I did, and soon I started to feel for my client and to see things from their point of view. Although the choice of the word 'unethical' was an unfortunate one that elicited a strong reaction in me, it must have been said for a reason. With a more positive perspective I started to appreciate that for this particular client the cost of a hotel bill and a train ticket is a significant one.

Most of my clients are multinational companies who are very used to flying people all around the world; that type of expense is just a part of doing business. This client is a small one that had been brave enough to invest in my speaking fee at a not inconsiderable risk to themselves, and had made it work. This extra unforeseen expense would make a big dent in their profits. So from that perspective I understood why they had the reaction they did and came out a bit punchy. Now I understood the problem, I was able to see a solution. We decided the best plan was to split the costs and make sure in future that all expenses were agreed upfront. Once again, all was harmonious.

When we get saddled with negative emotions that are not serving us we are no longer free. Only by confronting and analysing them can we release ourselves from an emotional burden.

If you're struggling to rid yourself of negative emotions, there are a few tricks that can help.

Next time that you sense a big negative cloud on the horizon, notice what is going on in your head and all the judgements and interpretations that are whirring around in it. In my case, what was going on in my head was this:

If he believes my expenses are unreasonable, he must think either that I am not worth what I'm charging or that I am dishonest.

He can't believe I am dishonest, because all my expenses are valid, receipted and according to my terms and conditions, therefore this must be about me.

If he believes I am not worth the money, then I must have done a crappy job because if my work was good, my expenses wouldn't be questioned.

So therefore I did a rubbish job, and yet I thought it was great.

So I must be doubly rubbish: first, at what I do, and, second, at how I gauge my impact.

If I am rubbish at what I do, I've been wasting my time and other people's.

In which case I'm a loser and will never be good enough.

And no one will love me.

So I will die in a ditch, smelling of gin.

We all have this kind of mental processing. The judgements and accusations may start out rational and with external focus, but pretty quickly turn into self-doubt and from there to self-criticism. Although in the cold light of day these thoughts look ridiculous, it's important to remember that a lot of these judgements are made subconsciously: we feel the emotional impact of those thoughts without even realizing we are thinking them.

All these judgements are designed to protect us. Remember the prehistoric brain's negativity bias, how it focuses on threats and danger? This makes it very easy to spiral into a deep, dark chasm. This whole process from reading an email to having an exaggerated, negative reaction takes less than a second.

Once we are deep into this emotional state, we need to clamber back out and see what we can learn. Remember, the first thing to do is sit straight, breathe deeply and smile. (I make no apology for repeating this often; it needs to become instinctive.)

When you are starting to regain perspective, take a look at the judgements and accusations that you were making and ask yourself which are valid.

Doing this will enable you to separate hard fact from judgement and conjecture. In the case above, we perceived my expenses differently: I thought they were reasonable, my client did not. What else was true was (1) that I had done some work for them which had produced positive feedback; (2) that I had incurred some expenses, none of which had been approved in advance; and (3) that they were running a small business with a limited budget.

The rest of the stuff in my head that was stimulating my violent reaction was just fantasy. By focusing only on what we know is absolutely true, we gain a rational and healthy perspective about what is really going on.

When I looked at what was true, it became a lot easier for me to decide on a simple course of action that avoided what could have been a car crash. Days, months, even years of fuming were avoided.

By regularly noticing what it is in your mind that is creating negative states, you will start to perceive certain patterns. For example the stuff that triggers me most centres on self-doubt, both in my own ability and of the merit of my values. I found that, after identifying these triggers, they began to wane and were more easily dealt with through increased awareness. What acts as a trigger for you?

We will always have emotional reactions, and 'Yipppeeee' for that. In years to come that's what will separate us from the robots. The question is, how to use those emotions to help us be free.

If there is something in your work past that you are still having problems dealing with, and that creates negative emotions, try this simple technique:

Write down whatever it is that is still annoying you, in all its gory detail, and be full of accusation and judgement, bile and vitriol.

Have a proper vent.

Fold it up, place it in an envelope and seal it.

For extra drama, set fire to it and watch it burn away. With it will go the negativity.

This might sound simplistic, but there's plenty of research to suggest that such techniques make us feel better about the past and help us move on.

GET CREATIVE

A major handicap preventing us from being free is our past experience. Every time we look into the future we cannot help but judge it by our past, so it is almost impossible to perceive real opportunity.

Our brains are amazing learning machines; unfortunately, as they learn they create models by which all new experiences are judged. That's why we often get so stuck in our thinking and trapped in a single way of working.

To truly break free we need a little creative magic that will provoke some fresh thinking.

I have spent most of my working life helping organizations become better at creative leadership, and I have learned that creative techniques and clever processes are not all that useful.

To think differently, you have to work at being different. If you act differently you will naturally see the world in different ways and break out of ingrained patterns.

Most businesses have a routine, and I would imagine yours is no different. Think about the things there that have been established for some time, that have become regular and habitual. Choose one you think is fundamental to the work you and your team do, and consider how you can freshen it up.

For example if you have a regular weekly meeting with the same people in the same place, following the same agenda and even sitting in the same chairs, shake things up a little. Change the time of the meeting, invite new people, get somebody else

If you had a blank sheet of paper, how would you design your job?

to run it, change the agenda completely, hold it somewhere else. Or start the meeting by asking: 'Why is this meeting so important?'

Perhaps there is a digest or overview that you all have to submit on a regular basis. If so, mess about with it a bit. Change the format by 10 per cent and see if anyone notices; if they don't, next time make it 50 per cent.

A friend of mine had to complete an arduous monthly report, with ten pages of spreadsheets and conclusions. After six months of filing this diligently, he began to question whether anyone was actually using it. From then on, all he did was change the front page by putting the current date on it and moving around the management summary, but never actually changing the content. He only confessed this to me after twelve months of mischievousness and receiving a promotion.

Challenge the norms and test the boundaries. You may well find that the things you think are important and set in stone are anything but.

Mix things up a bit. Dress differently, go for a drink with those Finance guys, clear out all those old files you've got and start afresh, sit somewhere else.

If you had a blank sheet of paper, how would you design your job?

No matter what your role is, there are ways to make it unique and special.

There is far too much discussion and debate in business. If you want to free yourself from that mindless intellectual pandering, do something different.

A close friend of mine, Jo Foster – founder of the agency Boom Innovation – recently found herself in a London taxi. As ever, she was chatting away to the driver, a gregarious and warm cabbie whose family were originally from the Caribbean; he had wild dreads and didn't stop laughing.

At some point they got snarled up in traffic and the only way the taxi could go forward was if somebody were to let them out from the lane they were stuck in. Surprisingly, a flashy S-Class Mercedes waved him through. As the taxi driver pulled out, he held up a laminated sheet to the driver's side window and smiled.

Jo asked what was on the sheet. Her driver showed her the card, which simply said, thank you. A simple idea, yet one with all the more impact because it was surprising. The man in the Mercedes smiled, laughed and waved in response to a gesture that set one taxi driver apart from the rest.

We can all do something that helps us to stand out from the crowd, that shows our freedom and what it is that makes us special, even in the most restricted of jobs.

Jo then asked the driver what he had on the other side of the card, expecting something a little more cutting, but it just said thanks. Apparently he likes to tailor his message to his audience: it's thank you to Mr Mercedes and thanks to White Van Man. Priceless.

Find one thing that has been frustrating you at work, and try doing it in a new and different manner (health and safety permitting).

If you were a guerrilla activist keen to shake up your business, what would you do?

What is it that you are currently known for in your organization?

And what is it that you would like to be remembered for?

What do you need to do to create that memory?

What can you do that you will be proudest to tell the story of?

We look at the unknown and our prehistoric brains see danger. Making the leap feels terrifying, but when we do we soon realize that we do not fall to our deaths but instead learn how to fly.

So jump.

notes

Go BE!

6

HEAD AND

HEART

As we've seen, being driven by our prehistoric brains is dangerous – they offer us limited options of fight, flight or freeze. But we also need to be wary of being too logical. One of the traps of work is to over-rely on our intellect to get things done. For many years now, business has all been about the battle of brains.

When we rely purely upon our rational and analytical processing, we miss out on so much of our potential genius. Logic is essential to successful business, but it really just gets you to the table. Recently there has emerged a very encouraging trend to redress the balance. It is not a minute too soon.

> 'You cannot analyse your way to ten out of ten. At best if you're smart you may reach six or seven but that will not win. The only way to hit ten out of ten is to make a creative leap.'
>
> Andy Fennell, president and chief operating officer, Diageo Africa

The challenge for us in business is to become more comfortable with delivering our work from our heads *and* our hearts. If we

Learn to really listen to what your heart is saying

listen to our intuition, we will make better decisions and have a bigger impact. Just as importantly, when we learn to do so we start to get balance back in the way that we work and in some way free ourselves from what has become an overly oppressive brain.

Just take a moment to think about the biggest decisions you have made in your personal life, the ones that have had the most impact. When you ponder those moments, how much of that decision-making process was intellectual, and how much was emotional? In my case, although the logic was generally solid on those decisions, far and away the most fundamental drive in actually making the leap was how I felt and not what I thought. And there are certain decisions I've made that my brain was absolutely baffled by, but my heart knew instinctively were correct.

Now take a moment to think about the decisions that have most impacted your work life. How do those stack up?

I love working with leaders who follow their gut instinct and listen to their people's hunches too. It's less scientific and rigorous and quantifiable than doing things by the book, but, if you learn to really listen to what your heart is saying, it doesn't have to be any less reliable. Even investment guru George Soros unwinds his trades when he notices a familiar back pain. It's his version of listening to his heart and it seems to have served him well.

After a time practising this you will notice that you will become more and more comfortable with the percentage of faith placed on your heart versus your head. Many leaders are happy to think really hard for 80 per cent of their efforts and just use the 20 per cent of their heart for validation. If you tune into your true essence, you might soon realize that those percentages will serve you best the other way round, as most of the good wisdom isn't even available to you until you've dialled in and explored it energetically. Yes, the hippie is rising.

CONTROL

I really don't like the word 'control'. There is something about it that seems pointless, as full control of anything can never truly be achieved. But a measure of control is important to freedom. To be happy, we need to feel as if we have some say about what happens in our work and in our lives. Even if the things we are in control of are small, they give us purpose and a place to express our freedom.

Daniel Gilbert, a Harvard professor, tells a wonderful story from the world of psychological research:

Half the residents in a nursing home were given a house plant and asked to look after it, while the other half were given an identical plant but told that the staff would be responsible for it. Six months later, the residents who had been robbed of even this small amount of control over their lives were significantly less happy, healthy and active than the others. Even more distressingly, 30 per cent of the residents who had not looked after their plant had died, compared to 15 per cent of those who had been allowed to exercise some control.

Similar research has been carried out in business. A 2004 study of small and medium-sized businesses in the UK found that those companies offering autonomy so people could control their own work, grew at four times the rate of those that didn't, and had only a third of the turnover of staff.

Some of us are fortunate enough to have roles, personalities or leadership support such that we are able to control much of our time and work. For others it's more of a battle.

In your role, what single thing would it give you a kick to control? It could be anything at all, big or small; the important thing is that it's something you can put your arms around and feel good about doing.

> **'We lost thirteen pilots in six months.**
> **And in nearly every case, the worst pilots**
> **died by their own stupidity.'**
>
> Chuck Yeager, test pilot

This quote from Chuck Yeager illustrates how fervently we need to feel some degree of control. Even when there was a mechanical failure, the general consensus of the fellow pilots was that the fault was with the pilot and not the plane: they should have checked it.

It may seem harsh, but if you are going to funerals and burying guys that do the same job as you, you have to believe that you are 100 per cent in control of your life. Otherwise you'd never get back into the cockpit.

We may not be flying planes but we can all take more control and feel freer for doing so. If we don't have control we can become unhappy, helpless, hopeless and depressed, and occasionally dead, says Daniel Gilbert in *Stumbling on Happiness*.

My colleague Andy once asked me if he could go and develop some business in Dubai. I knew he felt a tad itchy about his role and needed to stretch a little so I agreed, with two small conditions. First, that it wouldn't cost anything, and second, that he brought back three big ideas.

He achieved both goals, but more importantly, because he had freedom to do something he was excited by, his whole attitude changed. That project helped him grow his wings.

> 'If your success is not on your own terms, if it looks good to the world but does not feel good in your heart, it is not success at all.'

Anna Quindlen, journalist

Even if you run just the office Christmas party, then you have some area of control in which you can self-express and that gives you some freedom. Find that one thing, own the hell out of it, and do it the way only you could.

LOVE THE
DIFFICULTY

Michael Caine was rehearsing a play when, just before he was to appear on stage, a chair became accidentally lodged in front of the door he was supposed to come in through.

When his cue came to make his entrance, he shouted, 'I can't get in. There's a chair in the way.'

Without hesitation, the producer said to Caine: 'Well, use the difficulty.'

Confused, Caine asked what he meant.

THE
DIFFICULTY
WINS WHEN
WE LET IT

'If it's a drama, smash it. If it's a comedy, fall over it.'

Life is never all cocktails and massage, freshly cut grass and movie premieres, roast lamb or the first hot day of the year. There are bumps along the way, and that's what makes it interesting.

Those bumps can feel damned annoying – quite frankly, we often feel we could do without them. But they are integral to the human experience.

We need such tension for us to be aware of who we really are. If it's all plain sailing we never explore our full consciousness; we can just breeze through. When difficulties do occur – and trust me, they will – it's important to embrace rather than fight them. We don't have the energy or the ability to change everything. We only have the ability to change ourselves.

By embracing the difficulties and breathing into them and seeing how we can make that situation positive, we learn the greatest lessons and free ourselves from the fear of what may happen in the future: now its bite will be lessened.

Giles Duley is a British documentary photographer and photojournalist. His work focuses on the human spirit and the consequences of conflict. In 2011, while accompanying an American foot patrol in Afghanistan, he stepped on an IED and lost both his legs and his left arm. An experience as devastating as that is almost impossible for us to fathom. In a split-second he went from being on the top of the world and at the top of his game to a triple amputee who only just survived.

In such a situation, how can anyone possibly 'use the difficulty'?

As he explained in a *New York Times* interview, even as he was being tended by American soldiers immediately after the explosion, Duley went through a mental checklist: 'Right-hand? Eyes? I realized that all of these were intact – and then I thought, I can work.'

He believes because of this traumatic event he now has greater insight and empathy into people's suffering, and as a result can be a better storyteller.

The difficulty wins when we let it. When we wish it wasn't happening to us and when we don't think it's fair, we have lost. When we stand up to it and appreciate that it has been sent so that we can grow, we free ourselves and we find liberation easier every day.

'I have missed more than 9,000 shots in my career. I have lost almost 300 games. On twenty-six occasions I have been entrusted to take the game-winning shot and I missed. I have failed over and over again in my life. And that's why I succeed.'

Michael Jordan

CONNECTING TO YOUR TRUE SELF

When sitting at our desks, multitasking and under pressure to hit deadlines and targets, it can be a big challenge to connect with our true selves. But if we don't we will never be free. We will always be at the whim of what is going on around us and of our reactive prehistoric brains. When we truly connect we give ourselves choice, perspective and a sense of freedom.

There are many ways to connect to your true self. I have tried countless approaches including numerous meditation techniques, shamanism, hallucinogens and no end of esoteric practices, many of which I will probably never encounter again.

What I have learned through all the experimentation is that we are all very different in the ways we make that connection – what works for one may not work for another. That said, one constant is that it takes practice to break old habits. You don't become a great coder unless you write a lot of code. Equally, to make the connection effortlessly every day is something that most of us will strive for throughout our lives.

Despite this, we can get started on it incredibly quickly.

This is something you can do in a meeting, sitting at your desk or during a break. It needs to be part of your everyday work life and not something you can only do on the top of Machu Picchu.

A lot of the advice we are given when it comes to meditation is almost impossible to implement. We cannot empty our minds; there is no function key for it on our keyboard.

Thoughts and images will undoubtedly come into your mind when you relax, as your subconscious will start to flow with almost an unlimited amount of stimuli to process. Trying to control that would be pointless. For me the single most important indication that I'm connecting to my true self is a sense of wellbeing: feeling calm yet aware. The awareness stretches beyond rationality and into an altered state. It feels effortless when it's achieved.

Staying in that mode can be a challenge when you're starting out because it's all too tempting to float off and go to a rather pleasant but somewhat useless place. Our minds are not only easily distracted by all the worries and pictures that we create constantly, they also love to float away to a place of detached euphoria. Although the state feels attractive and it's great for a chill, we need to remain grounded to be of any use.

One of my clients recently struggled with issues in their business. There was an announcement about redundancies in a meeting and she couldn't make any sense of it or decide how to behave. It felt as though the world was caving in on her and her brain was yelling that she should just leave right now.

**Give this a try and see how you get on.
See it as a playful experiment and one that
can only help you be more free.**

1 Find yourself a nice quiet space where
you can sit comfortably with a straight back
and your feet on the floor.

2 Sit down, get comfortable and turn off
any potential distractions.

3 Sit straight so that you can breathe well and
the energy can run up and down your spine.

4 Keep your eyes open – that gives you
something to focus on and stops your mind
producing a Hollywood epic behind your eyelids.

5 Take in a deep breath and, as you do so,
smile. When you smile, notice how good it feels
to be doing this right here, right now.

6 Now it is time to concentrate on your
breathing and to make it as easy as possible.
If it's at all jammed up, take another deep breath
to release it and get that smile going again.

7 Now that you are starting to get your energy
twitching, feel the earth underneath your feet and at
the same time feel as if you are falling backwards.
Pay attention to the light above your head while
continuing to breathe and smile.

8 Keep doing this until you've had your fill.

Trying to gather some composure, she sat on a bench outside and started to connect to her true self. Within five minutes she knew exactly what she wanted to do and was excited about all the ways the game could play out; she felt that she couldn't lose. A speedy turnaround from being hopeless and out of control.

As time goes on, you can practise this so it becomes part of who you are.

LOVING
BUSINESS

In Part 2 we saw how important love is. In work we have the opportunity to act as a love machine every day. Loving actions are a conscious choice: we can decide to be functional without loving actions and just do what we need to do; or we can touch people's lives by genuinely caring for who they are and supporting them to be all they can be.

I love business. I love the cut and the thrust. I love the strategy, the branding, even those detailed numbers. It's all fun to me. That said, although it's nice to see a product that I've worked on doing better as a result, for me the real kick is to know that people are jumping out of bed in the morning, loving what they do and bringing all of themselves to that task. If you want your colleagues, team or entire workforce to be extraordinary, love them.

Jane Dutton, from the University of Michigan, investigated this: 'We found that employees who'd experienced compassion at work saw themselves, their co-workers and the organization in a more positive light. Statistically, they demonstrated more positive emotions such as joy and contentment, and more commitment towards the organization.' The results were consistent regardless of whether employees received compassion or merely witnessed it.

Love is the most sought-after feeling because it is the essence of who we are and what we need to thrive and be happy. We all want to be noticed and appreciated, so the simplest things can have the most profound impact.

A friend of mine has had a phone call from his old headmaster on every birthday for thirty-nine years. The impact of those calls and his direction and encouragement have made a huge difference to his life, just by sharing a bit of love and humanity. If love only happens out of work, in the evenings, the weekends and holidays, it's such a terrible waste.

Take a sheet of paper and write down all the reasons why you love your colleagues. Do it by individual and take time to make sure all those things that you truly appreciate are covered. Not only will this practice tune you into the lovable aspects of those you work with, it has also been proven to make you more relaxed and happy and can even reduce your cholesterol level.

Jo Foster was once travelling on holiday in the Tunisian desert. She was one of eight people in a land cruiser, the majority of whom were French or German; only Jo and her boyfriend were English. Much of the tour involved visiting historical sites and hearing a lot about the warring factions of Germany, France and Britain of yesteryear. The tour guide explained only in German and French, even though he was fluent in English. Although this started off as a little amusing on the first day, by the evening it had started to appear deliberately rude. As the days went on Jo and her boyfriend became increasingly upset by what they perceived to be a public snub.

They had some choices open to them of how to deal with this. They could get increasingly irate and do nothing but fume. They could have had a showdown and demanded the service they so rightly deserved. Instead, they decided to show some love and rise above what was happening.

At the next stop they went and bought three of the most glorious ice creams they could find and gave one to the tour guide. At first he seemed quite confused, but then realized how petty he had been – he had thought it amusing to behave badly, but really such negativity was pointless and childish. His behaviour changed immediately and from then on in he did everything he could to involve Jo and her boyfriend in the rest of the tour. One simple act of love changed everything.

Share the love and it will repay you a hundred times over.

And if you need more love, remember: get a dog.

Your Life, Your Team

Take a piece of paper and list those
in your life team.

How many do you have? Six; ten; twelve?

What about your barber/hairdresser?

What about your extended family?

What about your friends?

What about your plumber?

Time to start again: write down *everybody*
in your team, and don't stop until you hit
1,000 names.

Once your hand aches too much to write more,
look at the list and appreciate the team you
have around you, available to help you every day.
It's huge and they are there for you.

Send them some love and gratitude and
remember when it gets tough how many
people are behind you, helping you to
be extraordinary.

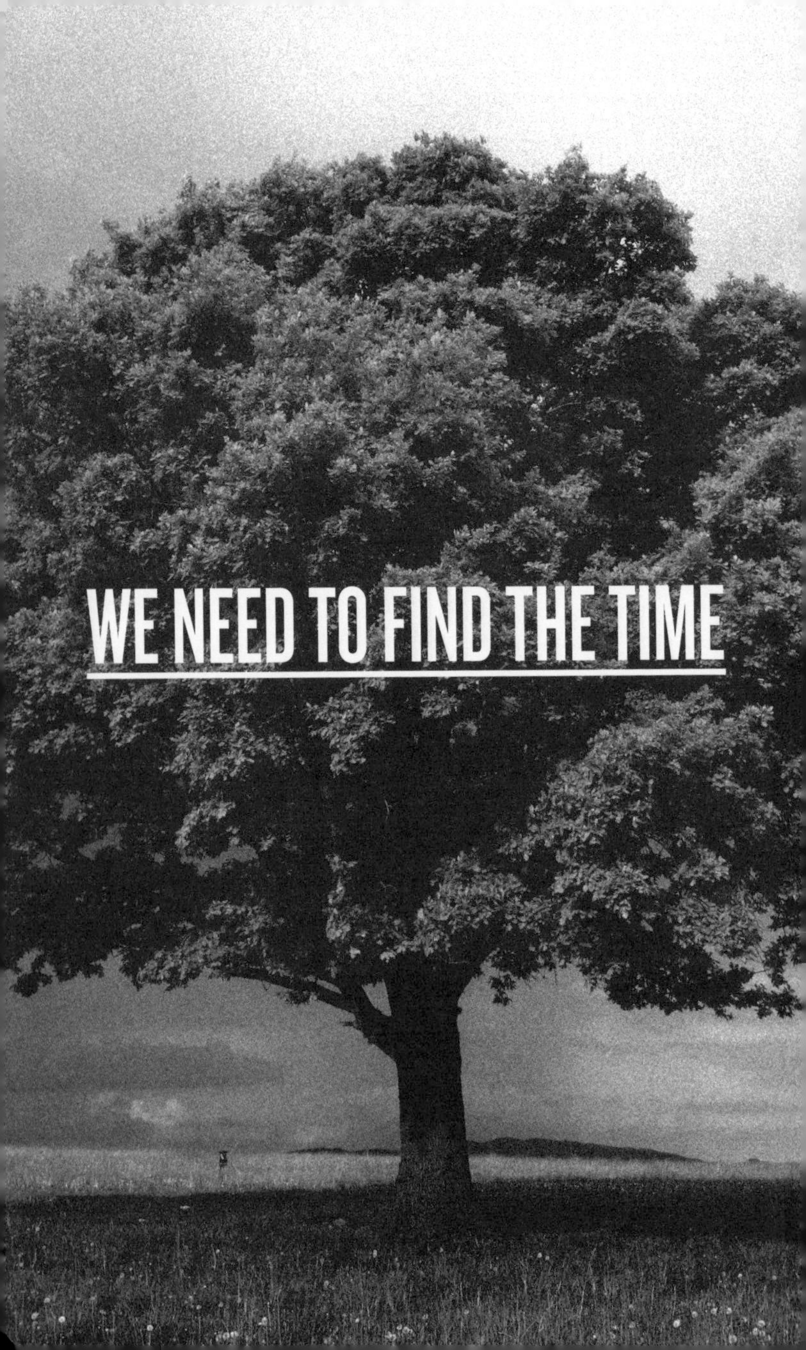
WE NEED TO FIND THE TIME

FREE YOUR
SPIRIT

Certain experiences in our lives generate more energy than others. These are the things that give us the highest returns for our investment of time and effort, though often they feel like no effort at all.

> 'Happiness doesn't flow from success,
> it actually causes it.'
>
> Richard Wiseman, psychologist

I went to the Burning Man festival in Nevada last year. Those four days gave me more energy, memories and laughs than any other four days of that year.

One of the dangers of our busy lives is that the good times get squeezed out, being seen as unnecessary or frivolous. This is not true. They are essential to us living our lives wholly and are a simple act of expressing our freedom that is healthy for us to choose regularly. Doing stuff for the pleasure of it can often be lost when we spend so much time doing stuff for its function.

When I am working with clients and I can see they are becoming slightly dulled, I ask them what it is that makes their hearts soar: what do you truly love to do? When they start to list those things it's as if they have just woken up. They become incredibly animated while telling me what it is that gives them a buzz.

These lists include skiing, painting, gardening, DJing, exploring historic locations, restoring cars, bringing to life their kids' science lessons in ways they will never forget, going to the theatre, etc. etc. When I then ask how often they do these things, their energy changes again and drops 50 per cent. Rarely do I find that people are doing enough of the things that they love.

We need to find the time and we need to make that extra effort to make it happen. It's all too easy to feel tired when we come home at night and turn on the television and vegetate. Every now and again that might be what we need, but it's not how we should live our lives. It's a trap that will eat you whole before you even know it.

I was once at a party with hundreds of people. It was a pretty boozy affair and at some point I struck up a conversation with a guy twice my age while visiting the gents. He seemed to have accelerated his evening slightly more than I had, and was feeling philosophical and a touch emotional. He felt compelled to share with me his life's biggest learning. With regret, he told me he had wasted his life watching television. He had a full-time job and he worked hard, and he'd fallen into the common habit of coming home, cracking a beer and turning on the TV regardless of what was on. He enslaved himself to his sofa and to mindless entertainment rather than to living his life and filling his soul with rich and meaningful experiences. Today we could quite easily substitute television with social networking or gaming.

I am not suggesting that we should never watch TV or game or network, but we should be selective and consciously choose to do so, when it is right; and that is generally far less often than we habitually do.

Do the things that you love and it will give you more energy to do great work. When we are happy outside of work, it helps us to be free at work as we are more in balance. Research conducted by the Albert Einstein College of Medicine in NYC has shown that reading reduces the risk of dementia by 35 per cent, while doing puzzles reduces it by as much as 47 per cent. For me the hero of the research, with a whopping 76 per cent, is dancing.

I once had an amazing run with recruitment: I was bringing in some fantastic people, all of whom were very different from each other but who all brought energy to everything they touched. I suddenly realized there was one common factor that united them. They loved to dance.

I am no disco queen, but there is something that is very good for us about losing ourselves in the music and self-expressing with some shapes. It's not about being good at it; it's just about letting go.

The stuff that really fills my life with joy is playing with my kids, talking late into the night with my wife, cooking amazing food, playing my guitar, walking with my dog and doing something near, on, or in the sea.

When I don't make any of these happen, I can feel it. I shine less and I find it harder to feel free and therefore to help others shine bright. These are not selfish things to do because if you don't do them you can't help others find their own freedom.

The Happiness at Work Survey (www.happinessatworksurvey. com) finds that happiness increases creativity by a factor of three. It also increases productivity by around 30 per cent, so it's well worth investing in.

In 2008 the prime minister of Bhutan launched his country's Gross National Happiness Index. He believed that conventional development paradigms were 'unsustainable, purely materialistic and very narrow'.

He explained that, 'in the end, the development must be about furthering human civilization . . . To increase and improve the level of human wellbeing and happiness. We are talking of happiness not of a sensory kind but also material, emotional, psychological and spiritual needs.'

What an innovation. Measure the stuff that matters and use it to guide policy. What would happen if you had a real Happiness Index at work rather than just an engagement score?

One small thing that has been shown to impact our overall sense of freedom and wellbeing is to spend time outside in the morning. There is something very connecting about it. Give it a go for seven days, and see what you notice.

FREEDOM FOR
WHAT?

No one makes you work. The choice is yours.
We also have a choice how we live our lives. We can
do the ordinary, or we can do the extraordinary.

The ordinary life is lived with the belief that what we have is all
there is. That life goes something like this:

*We are born, we go to school, we get a job, we fall in love,
we work hard and buy a house, we have a family, we work even
harder to pay for a bigger house and for our children's education
and for the bigger car we now need and for the more expensive
holidays. We need to be ambitious because we need more because
with responsibility comes financial pressure and the only way to
deal with that is to keep moving up and delivering more and be
more successful. When the kids finally leave the nest we can take
a deep breath and enjoy our retirement years and all that time
we suddenly have on our hands (better take up some hobbies or it
will be divorce). And then we die.*

For many that is the cycle of life, and the ups and downs that
are enjoyed in that cycle are enough.

For me, however, those things are not why we live. That is not the extraordinary life that we can live if we are free. That life goes something like this:

We live for love. We live for adventure. We live for laughter. We live for beauty.

We live for the moments when we are moved, moved by anything at all and for any reason at all.

We live for growth. We live for connection. We live to self-express and to make our own unique statement of what life means to us.

Those moments are our freedom.

There is no point liberating yourself unless you do something with it.

Today you get to choose.

You can carry on head down, working through the cycle of life, and no one will judge you badly for doing so. In fact, society will thank you for it.

Or you can look up to the skies and realize that every minute on this planet is precious. The only thing that exists is this very moment – not what you've done or what you hope to do.

When you look up and breathe deeply, it is fantastic to be you at that moment. Solemnly swear that every day you will reconnect with your true self and express your freedom by being you.

I feel most free when I am being me.

So be you,

all of you.

Be FREE.

ACKNOWLEDGEMENTS

My life is a truly blessed one. I live in the Paradise that is Lyme Regis, and since being there I have been reborn.

I would like to thank everybody who lives here in playing such a huge role in me feeling free every day and in helping my whole family keep getting away with living the most ridiculous of lives. You are amazing and I raise a cold cider on a largely inclement day to you all.

Upping Your Elvis gets to do the most fantastic work of helping people shine more brightly every day by loving who they are and what they do. We are so lucky to be able to do that, as nothing can be more fulfilling in my eyes. However, there are so many people to thank that create the loving vibe to support our work and I am grateful to you all.

The team includes the amazing Alex Heaton, Glynn, Clare, Heidi, Stuart, James Cloote, Jon Kilby, and many others who pitch in when needed. (Neil, that's you most weeks when the house once again falls apart!)

If food is love then we get far more than our fair share. Our courses are way better for your talents, so I doff my cap to the chefs and culinary masters, notably Tim Maddams, Gelf, Steve, Gill and all from River Cottage; Mark Hix and all his team, especially Jo Harris and Fran; and of course Alastair, Mr Spice and Rice (best damned curry I have ever had!). I am rounder and happier because of you, and I like it.

We all get stuck without inspiration. Mine is abundant and comes in the form of David McCready, guru to gurus, David Pearl, co-conspirator and enlightened being (check out www.streetwisdom.org to see our project together), Bodil Mjoelkalid, who has changed my life through nutrition, Kevin Jackson for keeping me honest (honest?), Emma May Morley for creative trifling. Thank you muchly.

To those brave souls who have played with Upping Your Elvis over the years, including ITV, Mediacom, Diageo, Unilever, Roche, Coca-Cola, The Nike Foundation, Gild, OMD, thanks for taking the leap.

I have an unfair amount of support when it comes to creative pursuits. My friends have been amazingly generous with advice, stories, ideas, feedback, hugs, giggles and general bonhomie that enabled *Free* to happen. Thank you to Jo Foster, Shilen Patel, Ben White, Mark Fowlestone, Stuart Hogue, Guy Escolme, Virginia Rustique-Petteni, Brad Warga, David Best, Andy Reid, Andy Fennell, Alex Dobbin, Richard Bravery, Paul Pethick, Simon Daglish, Andy Reid, Jethro Marshall, Maria Eitel, Archie (of Black Cow fame), Trevor Horwood, Julian Alexander, Joel Rickett and my very gifted brother, Mark.

Most amazing contributor award goes to Vanessa Barlow who has worked tirelessly to make this book great and keep me sane(ish). I really hope you like it as so much of your genius is in it.

My final thank yous are to my partners in Elvis, Jim Lusty and Matt Bolton. Without you guys, I could not be living my dream and leading the most extraordinary of lives. Thanks for everything, especially the dicking about that reminds me that it's all just a game.

And then to my partner in life, Anna. I am in awe. Thanks for having the faith and sharing more love than I ever thought possible. I am one lucky boy.